Getting the Fish to Swim to *YOU* & Keeping Them in *YOUR* Boat

Marketing Wisdom to Attract & Retain Customers

Alan Adler

Solander Publishing Company

Copyright © 2010, Alan Adler. All rights reserved

Solander Publishing Company.

This publication may not be reproduced, stored in a retrieval system, or transmitted in whole or in part, in any form or by any means, electronic, mechanical, photocopying, recording, or otherwise, without the prior written permission of Alan T. Adler. Brief quotations may be used in professional articles or reviews if proper credit is awarded.

Getting the Fish to Swim to *YOU* & Keeping Them in *YOUR* Boat
Marketing Wisdom to Attract & Retain Customers
www.gettingthefishtoswimtoyou.com

Requests for permission or further information should be addressed to:
Solander Publishing Co.
14600 Stonegreen Lane, Suite 101
Huntersville, NC 28078

Cover Design: Shane Amoroson – samoroson@gmail.com

Production: Lightningsource.com (Division of Ingram Content)

This book is sold with the understanding that the author is not engaged by the reader to provide or render legal, accounting or other professional advice. If legal, tax or other expert advice is sought or required by the reader, the services of competent professionals licensed to perform those services should be retained. The purpose of this book is to educate readers. The author shall not have any liability or responsibility to any person or entity with respect to any loss or damage caused, or alleged to be caused, directly or indirectly by reliance on information contained in this book. If you do not wish to be bound by the above, you may return this book for a full refund of your purchase price.

Library of Congress Cataloging-in-Publication
ISBN-**978-0-692-01075-4**

Special Thank You...

To all of the mentors who have given of themselves unselfishly throughout my life.

To all of the clients who have retained me as a consultant. You remind me that your organizations are the accumulation of people, technology and capital for without which there would be no entity for me to be engaged by.

To my colleague consultants: Ira Bass, Sherre De Mao, Andre Gien, Hugh Grey, Mike Hourigan, Dan Kensil, Jim Kothe, Dr. Terri Manning, and Peter Popovich.

To Marcus Lee, Attorney - Moore Van Allen

To Melinda Klein and the cumulative efforts of those who took their time and skill to make editorial suggestions.

Finally, I owe the biggest thanks to my family who have supported me over the entire course of creating this book. Thank you to my wife Mindy, daughter Sloane, sister Gayle and my entire extended family for your love, patience and encouragement. I hope I make you proud.

Forward

The most prevalent complaint I've listened to, during the recession of 2010, is that businesses aren't able to attract and retain customers due to the economy. In this book, I suggest that the economy is not the primary reason. Rather compounding conditions, including *choice, complexity and change*, are the more basic reasons why buyer attitudes and behaviors have changed so dramatically during the past ten years. I offer validation of this phenomenon and why "what got your organization where it is today won't take it where you want it to be in the future." Through case studies, I will present more than one-hundred sixty examples of *what can be done* and more than eighty of what *not to do*; if success is a key objective in your future.

The fundamental solutions offered, to diminish the effects of this marketing paradigm shift, include:

- *Pull vs. push* marketing and sales strategies
- Providing outstanding internal and external customer experiences
- Combining the *passion of intuition* with the *rigor of evidence*

As Ken Blanchard, (www.kenblanchard.com) co-author of *The One Minute Manager* said, "Although this might sound like common sense, so often I've found that common sense is not common practice in organizations today."

All organizations, large or small, in every industry can benefit from the concepts presented in this book.

Alan Adler, Author

Contents

Special Thank You iii
Forward iv
Contents v
Preface ix

Introduction 1
    Choice 1
    Complexity 3
    Change 3
    Culture 4
    Consequence 4

Chapter 1
Getting the Fish to Swim to YOU 6
    Birth of a Pull-Through Marketing Strategy 7
    PollenTrack 8
    The Benadryl Breakthrough 8

Chapter 2
Sharpening YOUR Message to Attract Customers 10
    Branding Philosophy 12
    Tropicana Sales "Squeeze" 13
    A Country Club...No Place to Rile Members 14
    What is Brand Personality? 15
    How Do YOU Define YOUR Personality? 16
    Why is This Necessary? 16
    Building a Relationship 16
    Tips 18

Chapter 3
Focus on Customer Relationships 19
    Healthcare Providers Lead the Way 20
    Walking-the-Walk 21
    Changing Culture 22

American Express... Approach to 23
    Customer Service
Tips 24

Chapter 4
Why Customer Relationships Matter 25
What Many Businesses Are Doing 26
The Case at Lincoln-Mercury 26
Alemite 27
Tropical Foods 28
Being Easier to do Business With 28
Tips 30

Chapter 5
How Easy is Your Business to do Business With? 31
Sales Prevention 32
Rewarding Loyalty 33
Mystery Shopping- The Customer's Experience ... 34
The Nordstrom Way 35
Zappos.com 36
Tips 37

Chapter 6
5 Steps to Improve Customer Relationship Management (CRM) at Little or no Cost 38
Tips 42

Chapter 7
Strategies to Leverage Customer Relationship Management (CRM) 43
Tips 47

Chapter 8
Getting Off the Crisis Management Treadmill 48
Tips 52

Chapter 9
Improving Business Processes Can Reveal A Gold Mine 53
- Boosting Efficiency and Profits 54
- Web-Based Processes 55

Chapter 10
A Truly Great Business Idea First Needs to Pass This Test 57
- Tips 62

Chapter 11
The Right Employees Make All the Difference 63
- Being Good or Great? 64
- Morris-Jenkins Company 65
- Nordstrom 66
- Overhead Door Company 66
- Integra Staffing and Executive Search 67
- Tips 68

Chapter 12
Competing, Generational Attitudes... Why Understanding Millennials Could Prove Crucial 69
- Competing Generational Attitudes 70
- Why Millennials Pose Such a Dilemma 71
- Issues to Prepare For 74
- Younger Generation... No Rush to Grow Up 75
- A More Optimistic View 76
- Tips 77

Chapter 13
Corporate Culture... Defining Performance Success 78
- Culture... Civilization in the Workplace 79
- Workplace Culture Test 80

    Toyota's Culture 81
    Zappos.com 82
    What Others Say About Culture 83
    Former GE CEO... and Culture 84
    The Bottom Line of Culture 84
    Tips 85

Chapter 14

What Got *YOU* Where You Are *TODAY* Won't Take *YOU* Where You Want to Be in the *FUTURE* 87

    A Brief History of Customer Service 88
    A New Holy Grail for Business 89
    "Pull" Rather than "Push?" 89
    How to "Pull" Rather than "Push" 90
    A Different Way to Think and Behave for
        Success 91
    Guide to Providing OUTSTANDING
        CUSTOMER EXPERIENCES 93
    Social Media Networking 95
    Social Media and Customer Service 95
    Social Media and "Pull" Strategies 95
    The Charlotte Fire Department 96
    Tips 98

Chapter 15

The Value of Internal Customer Experiences 99

    The Danger of Double Standards 100
    When Credentials Are Not Enough 101
    Internal Policy and Communications 101
    Employee Recognition 102
    Tips 104

Conclusion 105

Acknowledgements 106

Preface

The marketing wisdom found in the following chapters should in no way be thought of as breakthrough thinking. A more accurate description would define it as the fundamental price of admission for the company that hopes to create devoted customers. Without these fundamentals, breakthrough ideas are wasted on customers/prospects who feel frustrated and disappointed by the absence of customer care. To make matters worse, customers who are denied the basics become detractors of the enterprise. The lack of quality customer service rapidly becomes an employee morale issue. So let's explore the basics first and save the elegant for later. As *they* have always said "You can lead a horse to water but you can't make it drink"

Introduction

You may be asking yourself, is there really a need for another book about *marketing* and *customer service?*

If it's true that a picture is worth a thousand words then let me paint a picture for you. This picture is made up of five "C" words that look like this: CHOICE, COMPLEXITY, CHANGE, CULTURE and CONSEQUENCE.

Choice

To put it bluntly, we're drowning in a sea of choice. As Sheena Iyengar suggests in her book, *The Art of Choosing*, (www.theartofchoosing.com), in 1994 there were 500,000 different consumer goods for sale in the United States. Today, Amazon.com alone offers 24 million.

Have you looked for Crest Toothpaste, lately? Finding the basic "regular" toothpaste brand or your personal brand preference can be very frustrating these days. You may have to sort through more than 30 variations; and those are just the adult choices!

What are consumers to do when faced with such an abundance of options?

Sensing a critical need to fill, technologists have developed and implemented recommendation engines, as their solution to save people from drowning. However, as Lev Grossman pointed out in his May 27th, 2010 *Time Magazine* article, (www.time.com/time/magazine) "most recommendation engines are based on a technique called collaborative filtering, and it works on the principal that the behavior of a lot of people can be used to make educated guesses about the behavior of a single individual. Here's the idea: statistically speaking, if most people who liked the first *Sex and the City* movie also like *Mamma Mia!*, then if we know that a particular individual liked *Sex and the City*, we can make an educated guess that individual will also like *Mamma Mia!*"

Although Amazon.com, (www.amazon.com), was the pioneer of automated recommendations more than ten years ago, today, these filtering systems are also used by Walmart, (www.Walmart.com), Netflix, (www.Netflix.com), the internet radio service Pandora Radio, (www.pandora.com), Apple, (www.apple.com) YouTube, (www.youtube.com), and TiVo, (www.tivo.com), to name a few.

The article goes on to point out that one of the many problems with recommendation engines, as a solution to the problems presented by so much choice is that, "the weak link in recommendation engines isn't the software; it's us. Collaborative filtering only works as well as the data it has available, and humans produce noisy, log-quality data."

The problem with having so many products to choose from is not limited to variety and price, there is also another dimension... the immense growth in the number of businesses that market and distribute the vast array of choices available. This complicates the problem of choice by causing additional noise, clutter and confusion.

According to *Entrepreneur Magazine*, (www.entrepreneur.com), the number of businesses has increased from 22.6 million in 2003 to more than 29.6 million in 2009. That equates to an increase of 7 million more businesses in just six years, or 31%. We're also beginning to see recommendation engines to help people decide which business or organization to do business with.

The *Time* article also explains that among their limitations, "Recommendation engines aren't designed to give us what we want. They're designed to give us what they *think* we want, based on what we and other people like us have wanted in the past."

So, obviously there is a need for better solutions to this problem of so much choice, as it pertains to the myriad of products and businesses/organizations available.

The first implicit premise of this book is that the overall solution to the problem of so much choice can be solved by the people marketing their goods and services. The more effectively organizations "sharpen their message" and focus on their "brand," the easier consumers will find it to make choices they will be happy with. Likewise, happy consumers will tell their friends, family and others about the good choices they've made.

Complexity

As a direct result of the issues raised by CHOICE, relationships with customers have grown more COMPLEX. Pervasive use and improvements in technology have further exacerbated the complexity of relationships. As a by-product, many new purchase channel options have become available to the marketplace, notwithstanding the myriad of choice perpetuated by the Internet.

Video rentals are a good example. Just a few years ago consumers had only one choice…drive to the local video rental store. Today, in addition to the local video store, consumers can order videos to rent over the Internet, rent them from a vending machine at the local supermarket or, order them, on-demand, from your cable service provider.

Serious marketers have "upped their game" to remain competitive and manage the increase in channels so customers can shop and buy via the channels they prefer.

Change

The picture of CHANGE is a bit more abstract, but not by much. One only has to consider the overwhelming amount of crisis and instability during the previous decade.

Think about all of the change we've lived through between 2000 and 2009:
- The 9/11 Terrorist Attack
- The War in Iraq
- An Economic Crisis/Recession
- A Banking Crisis
- A Mortgage Crisis
- An Unemployment Crisis
- An Energy Policy Crisis
- A Generational Attitude Crisis in the Workplace... with four competing generations
- A Technology Explosion (including use of the Internet)
- The advent and rise of Social Media

Is it any wonder then, after considering all of this that, any person, family, business, organization or other social institution could go unscathed or not be impacted in some way?

Culture

"Culture...civilization in the workplace". Some organizations promote what their cultures are supposed to look like in the form of mission, vision and/or core value statements. Unfortunately, many but not all, are out of alignment with their purpose. Still other organizations deny they have a culture, which is almost worse, since culture is present even if it is unintentional.

The topic of culture is so critical that it commands an entire chapter all its own. If readers leave with no other message from this book, it should be that the culture of your organization will drive, determine and define success in the future!

Consequence

This refers to outcome. Good, bad, positive or negative. Readers will pretty much be able to predict outcomes based on the actions they take after reading this book.

The second implicit premise of this book is: What got you where you are today will not take you where you want to be in the future.

Consider the immense amount of change that has occurred in the past 10 years, then ask yourself am I the same person I was before? If not, then how have I changed and how have others changed?

Although many business-related books make their points (or draw their conclusions) using large and well known branded organizations, in an effort to demonstrate balance, the examples used in this book have been drawn from both profit/nonprofit and small and large businesses

While there are exceptions, perhaps you will likely agree that most of the marketing behaviors, concepts, attitudes and methods that worked well through the 1990's will not be effective today. So now ask yourself, what must I do to get where I want to be in the future?

This is precisely how this book can help. Enabling those who are ready and willing to listen, think and behave with an *outside the box* mindset. It can be a rewarding journey to negotiate this challenging era of CHOICE, COMPLEXITY, and CHANGE.

Wishing you the best of luck!

Chapter 1

Getting the Fish to Swim to *YOU*

In 1989, I gave a speech before approximately 3,200 members of the prestigious Information Industry Association, (www.siia.net) in Washington DC. The topic of my presentation had to do with how the company I co-founded, Touch Tone Access Inc., used technology to build relationships and help clients attract new customers. This was a few years before the advent or popular use of the Internet.

Prior to 1989, my company, Touch Tone Access focused almost exclusively on the magazine publishing industry and marketed a service called Touch Tone Ads. This service was designed to add value to a magazine publisher's ad page sales. Our automated service answered toll-free calls which enabled callers to select from a menu of options; including instant (audiotext) information, instant fax response, dealer locator service and direct connection to the dealer located.

Most magazine publishers used this service to replace the then common "bingo" card in back of many trade and consumer publications. Touch Tone Ads reduced the time it took a reader to receive information from an advertiser from six plus weeks to well, instantly, in most cases. A magazine publisher would offer their advertising clients, Touch Tone Ad service, at no cost to the advertiser, provided they purchased an additional page of advertising over and above their annual schedule. During the late 1980's and early 1990's, more than one hundred twenty magazines were using Touch Tone Ads. Although, we had no idea at the time, we were pioneers of what today is commonly known as CRM, customer relationship management.

Birth of a pull-through marketing campaign

In the audience and listening to my presentation, that day, were representatives from the New York based pharmaceutical advertising agency, Sudler & Hennessy, (www.sudler.com). They approached me afterwards and wanted to discuss how they might use my company's services with their client, Warner Lambert, (www.pfizer.com), makers of the popular allergy medication, Benadryl. Their client was interested in ramping up brand loyalty for Benadryl, in anticipation of competition from several non-sedating allergy products in the pipeline, which had not yet received approval to be sold from the Food and Drug Administration.

In a matter of weeks, my company enlisted 16 pollen level measurement providers and we set up a test to demonstrate that our Touch Tone Access system would work flawlessly. Sudler & Hennessy purchased television ad slots in 16 test-markets and ran Benadryl commercials, inviting viewers to call for the latest pollen levels reported in their zip code area. Then, viewers calling our single toll-free number were branched to the specific recorded information from their area, without any involvement of human operators.

PollenTrack

Based on the television schedule, it was estimated we would receive 35,000 calls to the program called *PollenTrack,* over a 16-week period. In fact we received that many calls in just two weeks.

To the credit of both the client and the agency, they didn't back off of a program that appeared to be going viral. They never cancelled a single commercial, because the program was too difficult or running over budget.

Stan Rapp and Tom Collins wrote about *PollenTrack* in their best seller, *The Great Marketing Turnaround, The Age of the Individual – and How to Profit from It,* (www.allbusiness.com/-marketingdvertising), calling it: "THE BENADRYL BREAK-THROUGH." In their book, they said, "The agency argued that this was a breakthrough opportunity to reach out and get involved with prime prospects. And the client had the flexibility and imagination to seize the opportunity and started shifting dollars from other programs to handle the flood of responses."

As a result, the client instructed the agency to expand the program to 50 cities and, at my recommendation, enhanced the *PollenTrack* computer program to start collecting additional marketing demographic information. We programmed our system to ask first-time callers questions about their level of allergy suffering, type of allergy they suffered from, what product they used when suffering, their age and gender, before providing them the pollen levels they initially called for.

From the information collected, we were able to split the growing database of allergy sufferers into multiple segments, then mailed those callers various level rebate checks and fulfillment packages, based on the segment they represented. Today, this concept is commonly referred to as *Target, One-to-One* or *Relationship Marketing*.

At the end of the *PollenTrack* program, four years later, we had:

1. Ramped up significant brand loyalty for Benadryl vs. existing and potential competition
2. Attracted millions of the 15 million allergy sufferers in the United States to "raise their hands" and identify themselves
3. Built a database of several million allergy sufferers that could be segmented by various demographic criteria
4. Created a mechanism for the client to frequently interact and enhance their customer relationships
5. Precisely measure increases in sales and market share, from a specific marketing program.

As Rapp and Collins concluded in their book, *PollenTrack* was a, "Direct Mass Marketing Success Story."

Chapter 2

Sharpening *YOUR* Message to Attract Customers

My colleague, Jim Kothe, (www.sharpenyourmessage.com) is a Stanford Business School MBA and former Clorox Company Brand Manger. He has also worked on brands including Liquid-Plumr, Kingsford, 409, NAPA, McDonalds, the (former) NBA franchise Charlotte Hornets and a family run business/NFL franchise called the Carolina Panthers. Previously, Kothe was also the owner of a leading regional advertising agency based in Charlotte, North Carolina before starting his own consulting business.

Jim Kothe offers a practical approach that includes 4 steps to help clients attract new customers and increase their sales by sharpening their message.

1. The client needs to answer the age old question of: "Who's on first?" Kothe even uses a clip of the iconic Abbott & Costello routine to make his point. A business must determine "who" is on first, as a way to identify a business' prospect. He says that, "understanding your prospect is the first step to sharpening your message and attracting new customers. Prospects are different today than they were just a year ago and must be listened to rather than talked to." Kothe implores clients to consider what prospects want to hear from the business.

2. Marketing GPS can help to stake out your position. Kothe asks, "Where is your competition? Where are you? Where would you like to be?" Lastly he helps clients determine "Where they stand."

3. Creating a clear VALUE PROPOSITION. Kothe uses the analogy of gourmet cooking, suggesting the need to "Reduce the SAUCE to the essence of your message," and determining the 'primary benefit/reason why.' The last part of this step is to determine, "Your FOCUS-OF-SALE."

4. Ask the question "Does your message FIT YOU? What is your BRAND/COMPANY PERSONALITY?"

Kothe suggests that every business has a "brand" although many are unintentional. He feels that branding doesn't need to be a painful process rather it is the most important way to attract customers. At the end of the day, the sharpening of a business' message becomes their brand.

Branding Philosophy

The following highlights Kothe's "branding" philosophy and uses a few diverse examples to illustrate the value of defining and then being faithful to your *brand personality*:

Symptoms:
Declining Sales, Consumer/Customer Confusion and Irritation.

Diagnosis:
A Case of "Brand Personality Disorder"

Tropicana Sales "Squeeze"

Most Brand Managers can't resist the temptation to change the package graphics, logo or both. It is human nature to want to put your mark on "your" brand. The trouble is, the brand really belongs to the consumer, *your customer*. Once they use it, and in the case of orange juice, they use it every day and buy it every week, it truly does become "their" brand. Therefore, when making any changes, it usually proves wise to make them evolutionary rather than revolutionary...and importantly, you certainly want to make changes that *reinforce*, rather than drastically alter, the brand personality.

Tropicana orange juice has learned this lesson the hard way. They recently made a dramatic change, which must have made the Brand Manager proud and the design firm a lot of money, but both are responsible for creating a "split-personality" for the brand.

As a leader in its category, Tropicana's previous look was distinctive; a big bright orange with a straw in it, as an iconic symbol. It clearly stood out from the sea of private label alternatives. Their brand personality could be described with words such as "strong," "bold," "distinctive," "fresh," "made from oranges."

They created a new look that eliminated the distinctive orange icon, used softer/weaker colors and had the logo in a sideways, vertical presentation. The new package looked like an imitation of the private label brands around it.

Consumers did NOT like the change. Someone had changed "their" orange juice! And while the juice itself had not changed, consumers have voted with their pocket book.

This dominant brand's sales suffered all because someone was more interested in change for the sake of change, rather than paying homage to the brand personality. Tropicana got the message and returned to their original package. An expensive lesson in Brand Personality Disorder!

A Country Club...No Place to Rile Members

A country club is preparing for its 100th Anniversary. As you might guess, the club is using this milestone as an excuse for a major restoration project. First returning the golf course to its original design, and then working on the clubhouse; a classic, white building with columns, looking rather stately with some southern charm mixed in for good measure. This edifice clearly needed improvements to its infrastructure and the kitchens surely needed to be updated with modern equipment. Unfortunately, a committee responsible for interior furnishings made a classic blunder. Failing to understand the principles of brand personality, they proceeded to create a whole new look/feel to several main rooms...not a restoration...but rather, a total renovation. For example, they chose modern, armless chairs for a very traditional room in a southern style clubhouse.
The inside must fit with the outside... The result was a minor membership revolt! "Look what they've done to our Pine

Room," was the response. (Note the use of "our." Membership organizations, like churches and country clubs, have a very strong sense of ownership among the members.) It was a clear case of the committee, either not understanding the brand personality or deciding it was their responsibility to change it. Whatever the reason, the chairs didn't "fit" with what the members perceived as the personality of the room and the clubhouse. The Board has not received as much member comment on any issue in recent memory. By the way, those modern armless chairs have been replaced.

What is *Brand Personality?*

Perhaps the easiest way to relate to this brand personality concept is to begin by reviewing the use of characters that are closely identified with a brand. These characters become the manifestation of the brand's personality. Historically, a good example is an illustrated character (like Mr. Clean) and a real person (the Marlboro Man). More recently, perhaps the best example is Apple in their "Mac vs. PC" advertising. In this unique campaign, they not only personify their own brand in the form of a real person, they also personify the brand personality of their competition PC; who always seems to look a lot like Bill Gates.

The contrast Apple makes in this campaign is about the differences between the two brand personalities, and by logical extension, the differences between the personalities of the users of these two brands. The issue of choice between the two computers becomes a broader issue than which computer system has the benefits/features you want. Consumers decide which brand personality they want to be associated with, and which personality they want to embrace.

Following that, Microsoft, (www.microsoft.com) counter-punched. Having been characterized by their competitor as a "geeky" brand, they began showing young children doing exciting projects on the computer, ending with each child saying: "I am PC." It's a clear effort to redefine their brand personality, on *their* own terms. Both of these ad campaigns reinforce the point that brand personality is a very important part of your brand/company equity.

How Do *YOU* Define *YOUR* Personality?

In addressing this issue with my clients, I ask them to think of their brand as if it were a real person walking down the street:

- Is it male or female?
- How is it dressed?
- Where is it going?
- Is it alone or with others?
- What does it believe in?

This exercise helps free people up to think about their company/brand in a different manner. The result is a list of adjectives that, when viewed as a whole, establish the "brand personality."

Why is This Necessary?

This is necessary because without it, you have no reference point to evaluate recommendations for your brand. Is the creative effort for a new ad campaign appropriate for your brand? Is this year's sales incentive theme consistent with your personality? Is the recommendation for your brand to sponsor an event "in sync" with your brand personality? All the aspects of your marketing communications MUST "fit" your brand. Otherwise, you risk sending a conflicting signal to your target audience, including your own sales staff.

Ultimately, we get to the real heart of the matter: whose brand is it? You may be the owner of the company, the Brand Manager, or the Account Executive at the ad agency...and each of you would refer to it as "your brand." However, you are not in a vacuum. There is another group of people who also think of it as "their brand..." the customer/consumer.

Building a Relationship

Branding is all about building or creating a relationship between the brand/product and, the user, the stronger the bond, the greater the loyalty. (By the way, the same is true of sales!) People refer to brands in the first person, e.g. "I'm out of *my* shampoo." A major factor influencing this consumer – product relationship, is the user's perception of the brand's personality. Consumers make a choice to be associated with the brand. The first encounter may be like a blind date…a chance impulse purchase. The consumer makes a judgment about continuing the relationship (a repeat purchase) based on the effectiveness of the product *and* their comfort level with regard to becoming associated with, in fact, *embracing* the brand/company personality. Another example is how consumers become loyal to brands of automobiles they purchase. Consider the loyalty of Mercedes Benz, (www.mbusa.com) vs. BMW, (www.bmwusa.com) owners. Remember, in the "World According to Apple," you aren't just buying a computer; you are also buying into their brand personality/lifestyle.

A Prescription for curing "Brand Personality Disorder"

So, it doesn't matter what you sell -- it could be orange juice, new furniture for a country club or your own company's product or service -- in all cases, it pays to avoid even a mild case of Brand Personality Disorder. And, you don't even need to take two aspirin. First, define your brand/company personality and then, by all means, be faithful to it when planning your next sales meeting, creating your sales materials, your web site, advertising campaign, and all other forms of your marketing communications.

Tips To Attract the Fish to *YOUR* Boat

1. Understand Your Prospects
   - They are different today than just a year ago
   - Listen to them, find out "what" they want to hear from you

2. Stake Out Your Position
   - Where is your competition?
   - Where are you? Where would you like to be?
   - "Here I stand!"

3. Create a Clear "Value Proposition
   - Reduce the "sauce" to the essence of your message
   - Primary benefit/reason why
   - Your "focus-of sale"

4. Does Your Message "Fit" You?
   - What is your "Brand/Company Personality?"
   - Who are we?
   - What do we like/dislike?
   - What do we believe in?

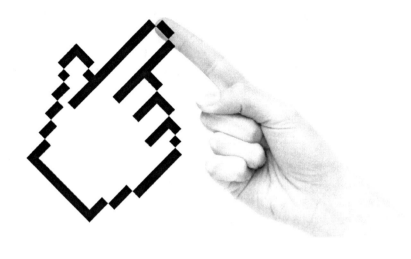

Chapter 3

Focus on Customer Relationships

Healthcare Providers Lead the Way

Leaders across various industry segments have been eager to share steps their organizations are taking to enhance customer relationships. One company that bases their entire business on those activities is Signature Healthcare, (www.signaturehealthcare.org) a primary medical care practice in Charlotte, North Carolina.

Signature Healthcare places a premium on access, individuality and patient-focused care. It does that by limiting the total number of patients admitted to the practice. The approach called "Concierge Medicine," allows patients fast access and a personalized approach to routine and urgent medical care.

For its business model to be successful, Signature charges an out-of-pocket annual membership fee over and above charges that can be billed to insurance companies for regular medical services. The fee also covers the cost of a comprehensive annual physical exam. This physical, says Signature co-founder Dr. Jordan Lipton, "provides the basis for an ongoing wellness program, managed and maintained by both the patient and his or her doctor. Concierge Medicine is not for everyone. It is for patients who put a premium on their time and desire a more highly personalized form of healthcare, in a more expedited fashion than can be provided by traditional medical practices."

Signature's 98% membership renewal rate is a clear measure of their patient's level of satisfaction. Some patients say Signature's approach places value on staying well – a factor they say is lacking in managed-care programs. Others have said they appreciated the periodic telephone calls from their primary care physician to discuss their health plan or to inform them of new treatment options for their chronic conditions.

Leading hospital organizations, like Novant Health, (www.novanthealth.com) in North Carolina, are also strong proponents of "Putting the PATIENT in patient-centered care."

At Novant Health, they have begun using *The Living History Program©*, (www.livinghistoryprogram.com). With this innovative, patient-centered customer service program employees and volunteers learn to interview patients for their (non-medical) life story. That story becomes a gift to the patient and family, while becoming a useful tool for the health care team. Not only does this process bring satisfaction to patients, who enjoy the process of telling their story; but the story gives the clinical team a mechanism to help care for the patient's heart and soul, beyond the diagnosis. Hospital staff is able to use the information in the story to connect with the patient on a personal level. Social workers and case managers also use the story to help in the discharge planning process.

Walking-the-Walk

The cold hard truth is that most business leaders talk the talk, saying that customer relationships matter. However, research suggests that there are, in reality, few who walk-the-walk... actually taking the steps necessary to change their culture from doing business the way they always have.

This reminds me of the saying, "if you always do what you've always done, you will always get what you've always gotten." Perhaps one reason for this is a lack of conviction by leaders to willingly and proactively address change as a positive within their organizations.

The chief executive of a manufacturing repair business shared his efforts to implement the popular off-the-shelf sales-contact software called ACT, with his sales department. When introduced and used effectively, ACT is a low cost tool enabling all employees, with customer contact, to share up-to-date customer information. This CEO shared that his outside sales people readily accepted the new tool, liked using it and did not know how they ever lived without it. However, the inside sales/customer service people refused to accept, learn or even use the software. The CEO did not want a confrontation with the long-term employees that handled this department so; he just let things remain the way they were.

This executive believes that sharing knowledge among all customer contact employees will enhance customer relationships and be better for the business.

Changing Culture

One business that talks-the-talk and walks-the walk is Livingston & Haven Technologies Company, (www.lhtech.com) a provider of innovative productivity solutions for manufacturers throughout the southeast.

This 57 year-old company has made great strides by creating a culture loaded with customer relationship enhancements.

Using a phased approach and measuring return on investment at every step, it began by converting their customer list of 6,000 to an Oracle database. Then L & H moved to sales automation, enabling all relevant employees to access every customer's buying history and sales interactions in real time.

"One unanticipated result we identified, after implementing sales automation, was a higher level of cooperation between departments," says Clifton Vann IV, company president. "In the past, departments worked in a vacuum. As an example, the accounting and sales departments would each have their own agendas, whenever they were communicating with the customer. Today, with the ability to share timely comprehensive customer information among departments, costly errors are avoided," Vann says.

Capitalizing on the premise that 80% of profits are generated from 20% of customers, L & H implemented a customer relationship management platform enabling it to segment their customer base into categories of *gold*, *silver*, *bronze* and *lead*. "The results of these efforts have been staggering.

"In 2005, 33% of our customers were in the lead category, costing us money to do business with them," he says. "Today, we have less than 15% lead customers. Plus, we no longer do somersaults for lead customers while keeping our *silver* and *gold* customers on hold."

"Customer segmentation has also led us to modify our sales compensation plan. Since eliminating incentives on sales made to lead customers, our sales people earn more money when spending their time calling on silver and gold customers," Vann adds.

This case exemplifies how changes to culture can have significant impacts on both customer relationships and profitability.

American Express... Approach to Customer Service

For more than three years, under the approach of its CEO Kenneth Chenault, American Express, (www.american-express.com) has been working on a company-transformation toward delivering outstanding customer experiences.

Out of this effort came a new employee training and a voice-of-the-customer program called Net Promoter Score. For the third year consecutively, J.D. Powers and Associates, (www.jdpower.com) has ranked the credit card giant highest in consumer satisfaction when compared to other credit card companies.

Jim Bush, head of worldwide service and others within American Express, created a strategy called Relationship Care, to further the company's initiative. They looked at the service environment and the number of interactions Am Ex has and decided to "make an opportunity to build relationships with customers," he says.

The strategy cultivates a personal connection with each customer, every time they contact the company. They also used this opportunity to hire employees from the hospitality and sales industries, who traditionally bring customer know-how, and invested in new technology that empowers American Express to increase their knowledgeable recommendations to customers.

Today, Beth Lacey, senior vice president of customer care solutions at American Express, says, "it's no longer about average hold time or how quickly its customer care professionals can get off the phone; it's how rapidly employees can solve customer problems and build a relationship with them. Anyone can learn the screens, but we're not in the screen business. Now we spend 70 percent on how to service customers and how to work at a company with a service heritage like American Express."

Tips To Attract the Fish & Keep Them in *YOUR* Boat

1. If you always do what you've always done, you will always get what you've always gotten

2. It's important for leaders to sell change as a positive with their organizations

3. Whenever considering a change, acknowledge all the stakeholders in the process

4. Segmenting customers can help you avoid wasting resources on unprofitable customers and pay more attention to profitable ones

5. Changes to culture can have a big impact on relationships and profitability

6. Look for opportunities to build relationships

7. Cultivate a personal connection with each customer, every time they contact the company

Chapter 4

Why Customer Relationships Matter

What Many Businesses Are Doing

Corporate giants have spent billions to improve satisfaction and build loyalty among existing customers, using most of these dollars to implement expensive "Customer Relationship Management," (CRM) systems.

CRM is driven by information gathered from every customer interaction. These include interactions from point-of-sale, web sites, ATM cards, frequent flyer/buyer affinity clubs and customer service/support. Corporations, municipalities and professional sports organizations use this intelligence to strengthen their customer relationships, capitalize on marketing opportunities and constantly identify new ways to be easier to do business with.

The Case at Lincoln-Mercury

Lincoln-Mercury, (www.lincolnmercury.com) General Manager, John Fitzpatrick, underscored the significance of the CRM movement when he spoke about his company's investment for the 2005 model year marketing effort. "We are dedicating nearly 25% of our total marketing budget to customer relationship events which represents a substantial commitment when compared to prior launches." These events included everything from fundraising to social media.

For years, marketing gurus have said that it costs 10 times more to acquire a new customer than to keep an existing one. Businesses of all sizes are becoming proactive and responding to this premise. In efforts to remain competitive and build loyalty among existing customers, businesses have reduced prices and added value to their products and services to distinguish themselves from competitors. Companies are finding that the same methods used to retain existing customers also attract new customers.

I visited with leaders across various industries to better understand what steps their companies are taking to enhance customer relationships. Here are some examples of what I learned:

Alemite

Alemite, (www.alemite.com) an 85 year-old manufacturer of lubrication and fluid handling equipment employs a combined 350 people at their southeastern U. S. headquarters and manufacturing plant in Johnson City, Tennessee. Their Director of Business Development described some of the many efforts to make the company easier to do business with. Alemite product marketing, sales and support staff are encouraged to work inside the plant annually so they experience production processes first hand.

"When people who design, sell and support the products, experience making the products, they get an understanding of how the plant functions and the value we offer to customers," the director says. This intra-company education helps ensure that customers receive a satisfying experience, when interfacing with Alemite personnel.

Alemite listens and learns from customers by offering several paths for feedback. In addition to participating in trade shows, they facilitate distributor meetings, training classes, and conference calls. Alemite also meets with end-users and provides a forum for customer feedback on their web site. As a direct result of customer feedback, Alemite built prototypes of a radical newly designed grease gun, shaped and sized like a hand-held, battery powered drill. Following testing and some revisions, the product was launched.

In just nine months the new product captured 60% of the industrial market. With this success, a larger more powerful version was produced to meet customer demand.

Alemite has also benefited by recognizing differences in customer needs, as they grow internationally. They said, "We learned that, in addition to cultural, language and monetary differences, international customers have different satisfaction drivers than domestic clients." For example, in some countries trade shows are the preferred location to order product rather than having sales people call on purchasers directly.

Tropical Foods

Another example is Tropical Foods, (www.tropical-foods.com) a 2nd generation family owned business that packages and markets a large variety of nuts, dried fruits and specialty mixes throughout the southeast. The company distributes its products, along with a selection of other manufacturer's candy and gourmet foods, to retail stores, hotels, bakeries, supermarkets and food service companies. Recognizing the need to constantly find ways to be easier to do business with, Tropical Foods' officials spent over eighteen months undergoing the largest revamping and reorganization in the company's 31-year history.

Tropical Foods president, John Bauer, says the company used the Jim Collins', (www.jimcollins.com) best seller *Good To Great* as a guide and textbook. Collin's and his research team spent five years analyzing 28 companies to discover why some companies make the leap to greatness while others don't.

The company's game plan was to limit layers of bureaucracy, integrate all of the department's customer responsiveness and avoid having their products being perceived as a commodity. "While we are never the cheapest, we have confidence that we're the best value with knowledge and solutions to solve our customer's problems," Bauer says.

From customer feedback, sales reps suggested including photos of selections in their on-line catalog at www.tropicalfoods.com. Results, since the change, indicate a 15% improvement in catalog orders. In addition to providing custom packaging and mixes of their products, Tropical Foods fulfills orders received by 11:00 AM, and delivers them the next business day rather than the 48 to 72 hour window, of the past.

Bauer strongly believes that it not only takes people to become a great company, it takes the *right* people on the ship to build a great company.

Being Easier to do Business With

Alemite and Tropical Foods demonstrate that being easier to do business with takes more than a person, program, reorganization or infusion of technology. It takes a culture with continuous focus on the customer and the customer's perception of their experience.

Tips To Attract the Fish & Keep Them In *YOUR* Boat

1. CRM systems can help with building relationships, however they are only a tool

2. Companies find that using the same methods to retain existing customers, attract new customers

3. Encouraging staff to spend (some) time in the plant or field, can help build internal relationships and perpetuate understanding of how all of the pieces work together

4. In addition to obvious differences, international customers have different satisfaction drivers than domestic clients

5. The importance of listening & learning from customers cannot be overstated

6. It not only takes people to build a great company, it takes the *right* people

Chapter 5

How Easy is *YOUR* Business to do Business With?

Sales Prevention

Making sure your business is easy to do business with is critical in today's marketplace, since purchasers now have more choices than ever. Why should they choose you? They will be more likely to choose your business if they don't encounter sales prevention. Usually, *sales prevention*, not poor customer service, is the primary reason for being perceived as difficult to do business with. Wherever *sales prevention* occurs, it must be identified and removed expeditiously, to minimize damage and impairing the health and financial growth of the organization.

It is easy to think of "sales prevention" and "poor customer service" as being the same thing. However, the two are mutually exclusive and should not be used synonymously.

Customer service issues are intermittent and can usually be improved with training, retraining, or changing a policy or procedure. Sales prevention is a repetitive, frustrating and annoying situation, perceived by the purchaser, which usually evolves from a well-intentioned marketing, cost-saving or other management driven effort. What makes *sales prevention* particularly insidious is that senior management is usually unaware when *sales prevention* is happening.

Sales prevention can occur in any type of organization, including non-profits. A few years ago I was consulting with a southern U.S. blood-donor division of the American Red Cross, (www.Americanredcross.com). An analysis revealed that more than 70% of inbound callers were getting busy signals. These calls were from potential donors, trying to find a location or make an appointment to donate blood.

To solve the problem, they needed to replace their telephone system with one that would automatically and efficiently route calls to all of their staffed positions plus overflow contingencies. Once this change was completed they successfully overcame a severe sales prevention problem. Additionally, shortly after the converting to the new system, the division was recognized for leading the nation in blood-donor activity.

Incomplete Web Info

There are literally millions of examples of sales prevention in the retail industry. One of the most frustrating experiences for consumers is searching a retailer's website for answers and finding the information difficult to locate or missing entirely. Recently, I went to a major retailer's Web site for stores in my area, so I could purchase a specific style of shoe. To my frustration, the state of North Carolina was not listed as having any stores – though I was aware the company has several locations in the state.

I sent the company's marketing department an email regarding the annoying omission, however, never received the courtesy of a response. So, I chose to purchase shoes from a different manufacturer. One who placed a higher value on courtesy and was also easier to do business with. In this case, the first shoe retailer not only lost a shoe sale, but also a customer's loyalty.

An example everyone can relate to

How many times have you called an organization, only to be re-directed from one department to another? That is, if you were lucky enough to talk with a "live" person in the first place. Automated attendant systems seem to have diminished or replaced customer service options. In many cases, the final contact may be a person working for an "outsource" company overseas, often with language barriers... frustrating the consumer/caller even more.

Rewarding Loyalty

When businesses become easier to do business with, they can create their own intangible benefits. Consider the San Diego Padres, (www.padres.com). In 1995 the baseball team launched a customer relationship management initiative, by starting a fan-loyalty rewards program. According to Brook Govan, then Padres' manager of fan programs and new ballpark technology,

the Padres saw the average number of games attended by loyal fans increase more than 25% per season, between 1995 and 2002. One change they made, well received by fans, was how they managed their lost and found process. Previously, a lost item was stored in any one of 20 different storage rooms in the ballpark. Less than 5% of items were ever returned to their owners. The Padres created a process whereby every lost item was logged into their computer system by item and location of where it was found. Then, it was stored with a reference number in a central location. Fans rejoiced because with this new system more than 75% of all lost items were returned to their owners.

Through this program, the team has been able to deliver a more enjoyable fan experience while increasing their revenue.

Mystery Shopping… The Customer's Experience

Any competent physician will tell you that before they can treat your condition properly, they first must conduct a thorough examination to determine a plausible diagnosis. Otherwise, they will just be treating the symptoms. The same can be said for diagnosing the "customer experience." The best way to evaluate whether or not you have a "customer friendly business," is to hire an outside group experienced in the art and science of "mystery shopping."

Mystery shopping is not by any means a new phenomenon. For many years, retailers hired mystery shoppers to come into their stores, pretending to be legitimate customers, to evaluate employees and report back their findings to managers and owners. In fact, this method is still the primary product offered by most mystery shopping businesses today. It is still considered by some as a viable way to measure the customer experience, via a snapshot of what the experience is like.

There are however, a few leading edge mystery shopping organizations that add many more dimensions to traditional mystery shopping. They are in the best position to help guide retailers and others with the most valuable intelligence, ultimately helping leaders make decisions and manage more effectively.

One such company is Ann Michaels and Associates, (www.ishopforyou.com). This twelve year old national business, is one of the most technologically advanced companies in their field, with access to more than 200,000 qualified, independent contractor mystery shoppers.

Company president Kathy Doering says that "traditional, snapshot views of the customer experience leave much to be desired when operating in today's era of choice, complexity and change. That is why Ann Michaels Associates offers a comprehensive menu of tools, to get the best three- dimensional views."

"Our clients demand a full range of services to obtain the most accurate picture of the customer experience, today. They include tailored roll-play, customer feedback surveys, social media monitoring, employee feedback surveys, and mobile vision short-form surveys that take advantage of cellular technology. This multi-dimensional view not only benefits traditional retailers, but also offers superior intelligence to insurance companies, medical facilities, associations, manufacturers and even health clubs. In fact, one of the fastest growing segments of Ann Michaels is competitive intelligence," Doering says.

The Nordstrom Way

Perhaps one of the greatest companies to ever promote ease of doing business with is the department store chain Nordstrom, (www.nordstom.com) reputed to be America's #1 customer service company. In their national bestselling book *The Nordstrom Way*, Robert Spector and Patrick D. McCarthy point out that, "Employees are instructed to always make a decision that favors the customer before the company. They are never criticized for doing too much for a customer; they are criticized for doing too little."

For years, business schools have taught and marketing experts have said that it costs 10 times more to attract a new customer than it does to retain an existing one. However, it has only been in the past few years that customer satisfaction has become a top priority in most "great" organizations. Purchasers have never had more choices than they do today. Competition, whether from the Internet or other sources, has never been more intense. Regardless of the term used to describe your customers (attendees, clients, constituents, consumers, donors, fans, patients, purchasers or patrons), businesses and organizations that overcome and eliminate sales prevention will always be more sought after and have fewer retention problems than those who are difficult to do business with.

Zappos.com… An Easy to do Business With

I leaned about zappos.com (www.zappos.com) by a referral from a friend. I was telling him how frustrated I had become trying to find and purchase a pair of men's "toning" shoes. It seemed that retailers throughout North Carolina only stocked a female version of this particular shoe. My friend asked if I had tried zappos.com. I told him I hadn't however; I did go to the manufacturer's web site but didn't make a purchase because of difficulty navigating the site and their shipping policies.

Later, I tried zappos.com. I found their site exceptionally easy to navigate, despite the voluminous number of 3,657,320 total products available in the warehouse for immediate shipment!

Not only did they have the make, model and size shoe I wanted, but they informed me that they still had three pair left in their inventory. In addition, they were available for $20.00 less than from the manufacturer's site. If that wasn't enough to demonstrate a compelling value proposition, shipping was free, along with return shipping, if I wasn't satisfied with my purchase, after it arrived.

Outstanding company… outstanding experience! (More about zappos.com's culture, in Chapter 14.)

Tips to Attract the Fish & Keep Them In *YOUR* Boat

1. Poor customer service is different than sales prevention

2. Customer service issues are intermittent, sales prevention issues are usually lasting

3. Sales prevention is usually far more costly than poor customer service

4. Reduce or eliminate sales prevention situations

5. With the staggering increase of choices today, outstanding experiences are key to attracting & retaining customers

6. Given the choice, customers are far more likely to buy and come back so long as they perceive your organization to be *easy to do business with*

Chapter 6

5 Steps to Improve CRM at Little or no Cost

Customer relationship management (CRM) initiatives are a proven way to enhance customer relationships, reduce costs and improve customer satisfaction. However, it is a myth to believe that CRM initiatives always require massive amounts of capital and resources. This is misrepresented by the fact that small changes--at minimal expense--can have far-reaching effects. Here are five simple, low-cost ways to improve CRM:

1. Call your main business telephone number and experience what your customers hear when they call your company

Senior management is often unaware how difficult it is for customers, who call their company, to do business. Many companies use automated attendants as a way to reduce expense. However, the menus and features of some systems are often difficult and frustrating for callers to navigate or to reach a live person to talk with, when necessary. Many consumers have experienced placing a telephone call to a business or organization, during their published hours of business, only to hear a recording instructing them to "please call back during regular business hours." This happens frequently when someone neglects to check or change a clock on a computer.

Menus can be changed or rearranged, and features can be added to the auto attendant to make calling your business a pleasant, not frustrating experience.

2. Create a mission statement for your call center, tech support or help desk that accurately reflects what's expected of those employees

When asked, customer service employees frequently report that they feel their job is "to make customers happy." This puts front line employees in the position of engaging in problem resolution, a task that may or may not be their responsibility.

A manufacturing client of mine was stunned to learn that each call, from end users of their product, was costing an average of $1,500 and taking four or more hours to resolve. Is it any wonder this company's technical support department had a 55% abandon call rate and an average on-hold time exceeding eight minutes? By working with this team and creating a new mission statement, more accurately reflecting senior management's desires, they were able to reduce the abandon call rate to less than 15% and on hold time to 1.5 minutes.

3. Turn your Customer Service "cost center" into a profit center

A necessary first step for turning cost centers into profit centers is the ability to identify and reduce expenses, such as lengthy phone conversations.

Here's an example: A consultant touring a call center was observing an agent/customer interaction. At the beginning of the call the agent started her timer. The agent courteously explained to the customer the reason for the finance charges and the customer's responsibility to pay them.

The customer disagreed and a debate ensued. The agent was polite but firm, and stood her ground, insisting that the customer pay the finance charges.

Four minutes into the call, the agent abruptly changed her position and said, "I will revoke the current and past charges," and quickly concluded the call.

Baffled by this, the consultant asked the agent why she suddenly switched her position. "At four minutes we end the call, even with past due charges, considering what it costs the company to keep me on the phone," she said.

4. Use your customer data more effectively

When a considerable investment has been made to gather customer information, you need that data to work for you.

Collecting in-depth information about your customers is not enough. You also need the tools and strategies to make sure you can use this data effectively. One way to do that is by focusing on data quality. Data quality requires more than knowing who is a Mr., Mrs. or Ms. It also means being alert for stale entries, bogus addresses and duplicate records. Poor data quality results in increased marketing costs (such as mailers that end up in the dead letter office) and potential misunderstandings regarding the true profile of important customers. If one customer record indicates 'Bank of America Corp.' (www.bankofamerica.com) with $1 million in revenue and another is 'B of A', with $200,000 in revenue, does your querying tool recognize the two as "one and the same" customer worth $1.2 million in total? Using your data more effectively can create real value.

5. Listen to your customers

There is no one better equipped or more willing to give their advice than your customers. Survey them frequently and ask questions like "how easy is it for you to do business with us?"

Discuss what they tell you with your managers and all of the people that interface with customers. Most often you will find that making small changes in the ways you do business can have dramatic positive results.

These are just a few of many techniques that can be applied at little or no cost to further enhance your business' CRM. Depending on your company needs, you may want to consider one of the many available CRM software solutions. Well-planned CRM initiatives can make a significant (measurable) difference toward enhanced relationships, reduced expenses, improved customer satisfaction and increased employee effectiveness.

Tips To Keep the Fish In *YOUR* Boat

Customer experiences begin with the basics. If those are not covered, the dollars spent will never justify the investment because customers will be lost, regardless.

To make sure that doesn't happen:

- Periodically place a call to your main business telephone number and experience what your customers hear when they call your company

- Create a mission statement for your call center, tech support or help desk that accurately reflects what's expected of those employees

- Turn your Customer Service "cost center" into a profit center by reducing or eliminating unnecessary expense

- Use your customer data more effectively by obtaining the tools and creating the strategies to use the data collected effectively

- Listen to your customers and survey them frequently. You can be assured that they are frequently considering your competition

Chapter 7

Strategies to Leverage CRM

The evolution of customer relationship management (CRM) software has seen programs add new features with each upgrade, and those features can revolutionize the way companies do business. However, experts also say these endless capabilities have made CRM solutions challenging for companies to manage, especially those organizations with only basic requirements.

To effectively leverage benefits that CRM can provide, companies must carefully choose the right software program and carefully plan effective implementation strategies.

Here are five strategies for successfully leveraging CRM applications:

1. Don't over-buy

A common mistake many companies make when purchasing a CRM program is to over-buy.

Feature-rich programs are often inappropriate for small companies. Large enterprise CRM systems may take two to three years to implement. Small changes may take months to make, which can be unmanageable for small companies. They can be so disruptive that people start blaming their poor performance on the CRM system.

But experts say software providers are selling small to medium-sized businesses expensive, large-scale programs, instead of recommending the program that best suits their needs. Too many companies, considering the technology, are relying on the software providers' consultants for advice, rather than independent objective sources.

2. Involve all stakeholders in decisions

As with most decisions in business, it's important to seek feedback from all stakeholders, when choosing a CRM program. That way, you can find the best solution for everyone.

The process should include feedback from the inside and outside sales departments, as well as the finance and information technology departments. CRM implementation involves more than just technical issues. When businesses make the decision to bring in CRM, management needs to pay attention to the cultural issues as well.

One of my clients learned this first hand. The company implemented a CRM software program but involved only the outside sales department in the selection process. Ultimately, the inside sales force refused to buy into using the software program, since they weren't involved and didn't see the benefits for themselves or the business.

3. Develop processes

Another common mistake companies make is to think the software is going to develop a sales process for them. A CRM application isn't the sales process; it is a component of that process.

CRM can do wonders for helping to manage relationships but it is the selling skills of the sales department that determine a company's success. Thus, it is still crucial for management to institute and develop a sales process before implementing CRM.

4. Roll it out

Complicated procedures are best learned in steps. This is especially true when introducing a CRM application. When implementing a feature-rich CRM solution, a phased-in approach is best. Organizations need to focus more on difficult areas and target exactly which functionality to launch first. Implementing everything at once, can be overwhelming and almost always leads to problems.

5. Segment your customers

Some customers are worth more time and investment than others. There are companies that lose money on 30 to 50% of their clients. Many businesses don't even know who their most profitable customers are.. As a result, the customer service and sales departments often engage in turf battles servicing customers who may owe the company money while the best customers are left with poor service.

There are even some industries, such as retail, that actually "fire" certain customers…notifying them that they are not welcome in that retailer's stores.

The ability to segment customers, identifying the most profitable ones and cultivating them, is important when considering CRM options.

Remember the company that segmented their customers as gold, silver bronze and lead? That company learned that 37% of their customers were in the lead category. Even after explaining this to the sales department nothing changed. They finally had to eliminate all sales incentives for those customers. Over time they were able to reduce the percentage of lead customers to less than 10% of their total.

Doesn't it make sense to spend the most time cultivating gold customers and little with lead customers? That is, unless they have the potential to be turned into gold!

Tips to Keep the Fish In *YOUR* Boat

1. Don't Over-buy
   - Feature rich programs are often inappropriate for small companies
2. Involve Stakeholders in Decisions
   - It's important to seek feedback from all affected parties when choosing or changing a CRM system
3. Develop & Use Processes
   - A CRM application isn't the sales process; It is a component of that process
4. Roll It Out
   - Follow a phased-in approach, making sure your staff is not overwhelmed
5. Segment Your Customers
   - Learn which customers are your most profitable and those who cost you money

Chapter 8

Getting Off the Crisis Management Treadmill

Often time's managers of small to medium sized businesses get overwhelmed operating from crisis to crisis. Although some in fact justify their existence by doing this. These people, for whatever reasons, will not take the time to create policies, procedures and processes. Nor will they implement solutions that would enable them to manage their businesses more effectively.

The following five questions can provide some help toward getting off the *crisis management treadmill*:

1. Does your organization have a communication policy?

A couple of information-technology people working for a service industry client replaced a computer server over one weekend. One result of their efforts was that on the Monday morning after the change, during the call centers busiest time, 250 employees could not access the systems they needed, to answer calls and provide service to customers. This resulted in frustrated customers, employees and managers.

Most people would agree that an email to everyone, whose work could have been impacted, in advance, would have averted this disaster. Clearly, better training and communication between departments could also have helped prevent this disaster.

The fact remains, that many organizations have policies covering core values, mission, purpose and vision. However, few have a clear, concise communication policy. When employees know who to communicate with, how and under what circumstances, the organization runs smoother and more profitably.

2. Can your customers be segmented?

Customer segmentation enables a business to define and identify customers by, among other things, degree of profitability. One client used to complain that, "our people do handstands for our 'least' profitable customers, while our most profitable customers are kept waiting on-hold."

Over time, the purchasing department began to segment and assign grades to the company's vendors. Vendors are notified quarterly when they repeatedly short-ship, over-ship or deliver damaged goods. The result of vendor segmentation has helped reduce crisis, reduce expense and improved productivity in the purchasing and accounting departments.

3. Is real-time customer information available to all who need to know?

If not, departments can inadvertently sabotage one another. One example of this is when the accounting department makes a collection call on a customer with whom the sales department has been pursuing a large sale. This type of event can totally derail a sales opportunity.

If the accounting department had access to real-time customer information, they could be warned of the sensitivity and take some other type of action, rather than making a potentially damaging phone call.

4. Are there manual and/or paper-intensive processes that can be automated?

At one time, I learned that a client of mine was generating more than 15,000 (unnecessary) paper reports annually. A clerical person was spending one week every month creating them.

The irony was that no one in the entire company knew why this was being done, yet no one was speaking up or taking action to end this unproductive and wasteful expense.

Finally, when it was shown how the one needed piece of information from the report could be captured via automation, 48 weeks of clerical time was recovered and put to better use, not to mention the many trees that were saved.

5. Are your company's databases able to communicate with each other?

If not, data is probably filled with errors and a lot of time wasted from redundant information being keyed into different databases. One client was able to eliminate eight database systems by updating and converting to a single system, which provided all the functionality of the previous eight. In addition to reducing crisis management, this change enabled everyone who had the need, to access quality information about their customers. It also helped management make smarter, timelier business decisions.

Reducing Crisis Management Offers Many Benefits

Reducing crisis in an organization reduces expense, improves customer satisfaction and profitability. Additional benefits include more productive and happier employees.

To do this however, requires an objective person; a term I like to use is "fresh eyes," to identify areas for potential improvement and facilitate the implementation of solutions. Making improvements like these enable decision makers to better manage their business instead of having their business manage them.

Tips to Keep the Fish In *YOUR* Boat

1. If one does not exist, create a communication plan
   - When employees know who to communicate with, how and when, the organization runs smoother and more profitably
2. If at all possible, segment your customers
   - While you're at it, segment and assign grades to vendors
3. Make real-time customer information available to all who need to know
   - Enable all stakeholders to use available information
4. Eliminate paper-intensive processes that can be automated
   - Doing this can dramatically improve productivity, reduce expense and save trees
5. Enable your company's databases to communicate with each other

Chapter 9

Improving Business Processes Can Reveal a Gold Mine

Boosting Efficiency and Profits

To achieve their goals, businesses need to effectively leverage the three major components of people, technology and process. Becoming more process-driven may be the most effective way for any business to reach the next plateau.

Some processes are informal, such as rules for how the telephone should be answered. Some are more formal, such as the documented process used to capture a new order. Processes are created to specific needs of the organization. For example, the process used to fill a new order. Or, the process used to run end-of-month reports. Many processes are used interdepartmentally. Such as when a customer calls in to report a problem with their telephone; a repair request is registered and a trouble ticket is generated by a person in the customer service department. The repair department uses that information to schedule and send a technician out to complete the trouble ticket. Although some processes like those in the accounting department seem different than those of the marketing or sales department, they may all depend on each other's input of information/data to function properly. That is why it's so critical that departments interact effectively with each other in a process-driven environment.

Many organizations practice "customer centricity." This is when the mission, vision and values of the business are designed around customer satisfaction. This is also a way for all employees to provide *outstanding customer experiences*. For organizations to do this successfully, employees are held responsible for cross functional responsibilities. With this approach, finger pointing is virtually eliminated and more importantly, everyone takes ownership of the customer experience.

Many organizations have business processes that are undocumented, redundant or not effective. When a process is changed managers often neglect to ask the user/stakeholders -- the very people who can make or break an implementation -- what *they* need to improve their performance.

Also, when outdated processes are replaced with new, more effective ones, the change can reveal a gold mine in productivity, expense reduction and improved employee-customer satisfaction.

One mid-sized service industry company engaged a consultant to help reduce their new order process from 28 steps to seven. This was done by eliminating redundancies and revising the company's method of capturing data. Imagine the productivity savings.

The best business process is easy to use, easy to communicate and easy to train. It is imperative for the people using the process to understand both how it works and how it is integrated with other processes. This enables the entire organization to work more effectively.

Key questions to ask are:
- What is the desired outcome from a business process and how do we get there?
- How will the new process function with other processes and contribute to the organizations overall effectiveness? If it doesn't, why are we doing it?

Web-Based Processes

Today, there are Web-based service-businesses that can cost-effectively provide, implement and support niche business process solutions.

One such company is Michigan based Process Performance Group (PPG), (www.teletracker.net) which was founded in 1991 by a group of former Chrysler sales executives. PPG markets a suite of process solutions that support CRM technology, to organizations which make and receive high volumes of telephone calls – such as auto dealers and realtors – each who face increasing competition and cannot afford to miss even one sales opportunity.

PPG's model for auto dealers is based on the fact that eighty percent of its business involves using the telephone. In most cases, they don't sell vehicles over the phone. So the dealer's objective is to increase the volume of prospects into the showroom. This becomes the desired outcome.

To achieve this outcome, PPG offers a service called TeleTracker. TeleTracker traces all telephone calls and the numbers used for dialing them to the ad source, and each is automatically recorded.

This process enables managers to do several things that, when all working together, improve the professionalism and profitably of their business.

First, the recorded telephone calls between prospects and sales people are evaluated and scored. Sales people are given feedback and training, based on actual performance. They're encouraged to reduce talk-time and use words designed to get the caller into the showroom.

Missed calls are automatically captured. If a caller hangs up before being answered, the manager is emailed a report with information about the missed call. With TeleTracker, a missed telephone call never has to be lost to competition.

In addition, TeleTracker provides automated reports measuring the effectiveness of a dealer's advertising. These reports are used by managers to make smarter, more cost effective, media buying decisions.

PPG services that integrate with TeleTracker are Lead-Tracker and Life Cycle Manager. Using Life Cycle Manager, businesses can track and manage the entire life cycle of their relationship with every customer.

PPG's client list includes more than one hundred auto dealerships and fifty plus large realty associations.

One of their earliest clients, Golling Chrysler/ Jeep/Dodge, in Michigan, won Chrysler's prestigious Dealer of the Year Award for its category.

Many businesses don't pay much attention to the value of retaining existing customers, yet spend fortunes recruiting new ones.

Smart businesses are finding a gold mine when upgrading and integrating business-process solutions. Solutions such as these can improve both the functioning of an organization and the satisfaction and loyalty of customers.

Chapter 10

A Truly Great Business Idea First Needs to Pass This Test

Admittedly, not everyone is content working for an established business or other organization. For those people, and others still cultivating a dream of starting their own business, you need to ask yourself some questions. If you don't pass this test it doesn't necessarily mean you don't have great idea, instead, it means there is more work to be done before you spend money and other resources. However, if you pass, your odds for success increase by using the concepts suggested in this book.

Don't invest energy and money in a venture until you evaluate the market.

I am continually amazed by people who think that they can start a new venture, say a restaurant, in the exact same location that at least ten others before them tried and failed miserably; yet somehow believe they can be successful.

You've probably listened to or considered many new business ideas. How do you evaluate whether or not an idea has merit? Most new business ideas are neither great nor new, and the pursuit of unproven business ideas can consume considerable amounts of time and money.

A few years ago I created a process to quickly help distinguish between the great business idea and the waste-of-time idea. I have used it many times to assess the value of such ideas. Sometimes the process has helped point out flaws or issues that had not been well thought out. Other times, the experience of working through the process has caused people to re-evaluate their interest in pursuing the idea entirely. If you have a great business idea, or would like to provide some good advice the next time someone tells you about an idea, ask the following questions:

1. Is there a market for your great business idea?

Many great business ideas have no legitimate market willing to purchase or use it. If there is no market, or only a limited market for the idea, then why spend time and resources on a concept that offers a limited return on your investment? There are exceptions, of course, such as the iPod, iPhone and iPad. However, there are few people who have the market producing clout and resources of Steve Jobs and Apple Computer.

2. Can the great idea be promoted and marketed?

Many business ideas cannot pass this test of reasonability. If the idea cannot be promoted or marketed, you may as well stop here. Once, after asking a client this question about his great idea for a new business, he realized that no media venue would accept an ad for the business. I asked him to consider the likelihood of getting media sources to change their practices in order to accept his advertisement. I further asked if he could reposition or restate the concept in order to generate an ad that media would find acceptable. The client came to his own conclusion and decided not to spend any more time on it.

3. Can the great business idea be sold? If so, via what channels and at what cost?

Among the most important decisions for entrepreneurs to consider is, can our great idea be sold and if so, via what channels and at what cost.

Some methods include: Wholesale, retail, third party, Internet, direct, multi-level, mail order, direct mail, catalog, resellers, kiosks as well as others.

Each method has benefits, costs and limitations. Regardless, entrepreneur's need "plan B's," or risk losing everything invested.

Initial financing is one thing required to get going, however, serious consideration has to be given to "what ifs." What if you have someone produce a quantity of 5,000 of your product with the thought that this is a "sure thing to sell out," but it doesn't work out that way? Or, the demand is so great that you sell out quicker than planned? Will you be able to replenish supply quickly? Each of these scenarios has to be thought through. Each has to be considered with a contingency to minimize exposure you're not prepared for.

Service providers are the same but different. They need to be able to expand or contract their business as necessary. The service sector world calls this "scalability."

Sometimes, after considering the answers to this question, the conclusion reached is that there is no practical or cost effective sales channel to sell the idea. However, if there is a proven market and sales channel to sell the concept, then you should continue answering the next four questions.

4. Can the great business idea be delivered?

No business should ever be caught in the situation of selling something they can't deliver. People who have tried doing this were ultimately convicted of felonies and ended up serving time in prison.

A client once told me about an idea he had for providing traffic information by *location on demand*. This great idea met the first three criteria. However, after considering how much it would cost to buy the information from a third party or create an infrastructure to obtain the information; the cost turned out to be prohibitive. That great idea was killed right then and there. Additionally, it is never too early to consider potential avenues for raising capital to fund a new business idea.

5. How will the great idea be serviced and maintained?

The importance of planning and taking the time to develop a plan that provides for contingencies cannot be overstressed.

Every worthwhile business plan builds in a layer of comfort, for investors, with solutions to problems that will occur with the delivery of the new product or service. If there is no reliable, cost effective back-up plan, then stop here until practical solutions are created.

6. Can you charge for the great idea?

Many great business ideas fall apart at this stage. Any idea that is worth the investment of time and money should be billed at the time of sale, or immediately after delivery. It doesn't make sense to promote market, sell, deliver and maintain a product or service that cannot be reliably billed or invoiced.

7. Can the bill or invoice for the new product or service be collected?

At this point, if your business idea passed the six questions above, yet there is uncertainty as to the viability to collect for what has been sold, I would suggest not wasting another minute, until this make-or-break component can be resolved.

Frequently, after people have answered the above questions, they are surprised how many details have not been thought through and the amount of work it takes to be successful with a new business venture. By now, you may think I am just pointing out the negatives and your business idea will be the "exception." After all, "with time don't all things work out?" Don't take my word for it; simply consider the small number of businesses started that celebrate a second anniversary.

People get passionate and excited when they have new ideas. However, they seldom drill down to consider all of the details and issues required to ensure success. Every new business idea must be evaluated, researched and rigorously tested. This simple process can help identify areas that need more work; and that additional work at the outset, will save time, energy, money, disappointment and relationships. Believe me!

TIPS TO SUCCEED

1. Is there a market for your great business idea?

2. Can the great business idea be promoted and marketed? If so, what is the cost?

3. Can the great idea be sold? If so via what channel(s) and at what cost?

4. Can the great business idea be delivered let alone, without the risk of committing a felony?

5. My Dad used to tell me that, "there was no amount of money worth breaking the law, going to jail or ruining your reputation for."

6. How will the great idea be serviced or maintained? If this has not been thought through, go back to the drawing board until you have a viable plan.

7. Can you charge for the great idea? If yes, what is the right amount?

8. Can the bill or invoice for the new product or service be collected?

9. As they say, "you don't have anything until the money is in the bank!"

Chapter 11

The *Right* Employees Make All the Difference

I don't expect readers to agree with every point in this book however; surely we can all agree that high quality customer relationships are at the heart of business success. The most effective way to enhance relationships and increase profits is by improving an organization's use of technology and human resources.

However, simply having people to do the work is not enough.

Being Good or Great?

Jim Collins, author of the best-selling book, *Good To Great*, (www.jimcollins.com) says that great companies "reject the old adage that people are your most important asset. The *right* people are."

Collins spent five years analyzing 28 companies, to discover why some companies make the leap to greatness while others don't. In choosing the *right* people, he says, "great companies place greater weight on character attributes, than on specific educational background, practical skills, specialized knowledge or work experience. They view these traits as more teachable, whereas character, work ethic, basic intelligence, dedication and values are more ingrained."

"If a company has the right employees, the problem of how to motivate and manage people largely goes away. The right people don't need to be tightly managed or fired up; they will be self-motivated by the inner drive to produce the best results." Conversely, he says, "If you have the wrong people... it doesn't matter... you still won't have a great company. Great vision without great people is irrelevant."

Furthermore, regarding executive compensation, Collins writes, "It's not how you compensate your executives, it's which executives you have to compensate in the first place. If you have the right executives on the bus, they will do everything within their power to build a great company, not because of what they will 'get' for it, but because they simply cannot imagine settling for anything less. Their moral code requires building excellence for its own sake, and you're no more likely to change that with a compensation package than you're likely to affect whether they breathe. Great companies understand a simple truth: The right people will do the right things and deliver the best results they're capable of, regardless of the incentive system."

Collins suggested the importance of clarifying the distinction between ruthless cultures and rigorous cultures, and believes that the distinction is crucial. He writes, "To be ruthless means hacking and cutting, especially in difficult times, or firing people without any thoughtful consideration. To be rigorous means consistently applying exacting standards at all times and at all levels, especially in upper management. To be rigorous, not ruthless, means that the best people need not worry about their positions and can concentrate fully on their work."

Lastly, Collins writes that, "Letting the wrong people hang around is unfair to all the right people, as they inevitably find themselves compensating for the inadequacies of the wrong people. Worse, it can drive away the best people. Strong performers are intrinsically motivated by performance, and when they see their efforts impeded by carrying extra weight, they eventually become frustrated."

Having the right employees has little to do with degrees or places of previous employment. The right employees exhibit a passion and willingness to learn, a strong work ethic, and loyalty…loyalty to you and to the organization.

Morris-Jenkins Company

Consider Morris-Jenkins, (www.morrisjenkins.com) the North Carolina heating and cooling company. Dewey Jenkins, president, says "When I purchased the thirty-two year old Morris Heating and Cooling Co., in 1990, we had only two technicians and six installers. I had no knowledge of the heating and cooling industry. I believed, however, that with the right people adhering to our mission and core values, Morris Jenkins could be the best company in its field."

Today, with more than 100 employees, Morris-Jenkins has an ongoing need for skilled technicians. "Our company never hires on the basis of technical skills alone, but rather hires people who are competent in strong interpersonal relations," Jenkins says. "We can teach the right person the technical skills to do the job. However, we can't teach the most highly skilled technicians how to get along with people."

Morris-Jenkins' people demonstrate their motivation and enthusiasm by continually raising the bar on their own performance. Repeatedly, the company has been recognized by the Chamber of Commerce with *The Amazing Customer Service Award* and recently by the Society of Financial Service Professionals with the *Charlotte Ethics in Business Award*.

Nordstrom

Perhaps no other company outwardly practices a "people" philosophy better than Nordstrom, (www.nordstrom.com); which may be why most customer service experts point to this department store chain, when it comes to hiring. In their book *The Nordstrom Way*, Robert Spector and Patrick D. McCarthy point out that, "Nordstrom would rather hire nice people and teach them to sell, than hire salespeople and teach them to be nice. Nordstrom, it is said, 'hires the smile and trains the skill,"

Overhead Door Company

Another example is Overhead Door Company, (www.ohdcharlotte.com) of Charlotte, North Carolina. In 1994, when James Potts and Randy Burris purchased the fifty-nine year old business, the company was managing 12 installations per day and averaging about $2 million in revenue.

ODC president, James Potts, says, "When we took over we noticed that prospects were calling constantly. However, our people were not enthusiastic, were not engaging the prospects, or working to overcome objections. Today with the right people and the training in place to back them up, we have increased installations to over 100 per day, reduced employee turnover and generate almost $20 million in annual revenue."

Overhead Door's use of technology has also helped the company enhance customer relationships. All trucks are now equipped with GPS, helping dispatchers increase speed of service.

Potts also credits the company's success to a culture that perpetuates honesty, integrity, fast resolution to complaints and the rapid return of all phone calls.

Integra Staffing and Executive Search

How do you avoid hiring the wrong people? Here are some suggestions from Michelle Fish, a 19-year veteran recruiter and CEO of Integra Staffing and Executive Search, (www.integra-taffing.com).

"One mistake is not thoroughly checking references," she says. "Companies feel that background checks, drug testing and credit checks (when applicable) are enough. However, statistics demonstrate that one out of every three resumes contain 'white lies.' If you are accountable for your hiring decision, you need to do your own reference checks. It is always a good practice to talk with others who know the candidate. Be sure to look for consistencies in the references and the interview," says Fish.

Another common mistake, she says, "is not having a detailed job description or performance requirements. Shortcuts during this process almost always result in hiring the wrong person. The process to find the right person for the job requires well thought-out character attribute and performance-based questions that are asked and answered."

Lastly, a (vital) consideration is the importance of hiring people who are a good cultural match; however, we'll discuss the importance of this more in a future chapter.

Organizations that hire the right people and let the wrong people go, experience increased profitability through lower employee turnover, improved customer relationships and are easier to do business with.

Tips To Keep the Fish In *YOUR* Boat

1. Hiring people is not enough, hiring the *right* people becomes your most important asset
2. The *right* people don't need to be tightly managed, they will be self-motivated and produce the best results
3. Technical skills can be taught, however, you can't teach people the importance of, or how to get along with people
4. With the right people and training to back them up, profitable growth is inevitable
5. Achieving success is far more realistic when there is a culture that perpetuates honesty, integrity, fast resolution to complaints and rapid return of phone calls
6. Thoroughly check all references
7. Be sure to have detailed job descriptions with performance requirements
8. Shortcuts during the hiring process will almost always result in hiring the wrong person
9. Hiring the right people can result in increased profitability, lower turnover, better customer relationships and being easier to do business with

Chapter 12

Competing Generational Attitudes in the Workplace… Why Understanding the Millennial Generation Could Prove Crucial

While the topic of the *right* people is still fresh in your mind, from the previous chapter, it would be valuable to look at one of the most serious issues facing businesses and organizations today…Competing Generational Attitudes.

Competing Generational Attitudes

For the first time, in modern history, businesses and organizations are confronted with four unique generations in the workplace, at the same time; The Veteran Generation, Baby-Boomers, Gen Xrs and Millennials working side by side, all trying to advance an agenda relevant only to them.

If not approached with some degree of sensitivity, herein, as some say, "is an accident looking for a place to happen;" an opportunity for unhappy employees, sabotage, turnover and a culture that will make it impossible to provide the customer with an outstanding experience.

Back in 2008, we we're told to prepare for the exit of the working Baby Boomer Generation. We were warned that they would be retiring and exiting the work force, leaving an enormous vacuum of experience and intelligence. Today, as we know, what was predicted just didn't happen.

For economic reasons, Baby Boomers have delayed retirement, largely because their devalued 401k's and other investments were decimated by the recession of 2009/10. It is now estimated, that this recent series of economic events could add as many as ten *additional* years of work, before a person who is sixty years old today will be able to retire.

Not only does this mean that Baby Boomers will continue to be "a force to be reckoned with," they will have to compete with the Veteran Generation, Xrs and the newbie's to the workforce, Generation Y, also referred to as the Millennial generation.

If these were simply names or labels you might ask "what's the big deal?" Remember, these are four different groups of people who are competing for positions, attention and the right to be listened to. Worse yet, each of these unique groups believe staunchly that, based upon their own core values, they are correct in their thinking and that others are wrong.

Why Millennials Pose Such a Dilemma

The 81 million Millennials, born between 1982 and 2002, (100 million plus, if you take into account immigration), represent the largest demographic group with the same set of core values, ever being brought to the job market in the same period of time.

They're labeled Millennials because their births cross over the millennial year, 2000. Behind the 84 million Baby Boomers this group is the largest generation. Therefore, it is critical to understand what drives their goals, desires and ambitions -- particularly since they will be the dominant group of employees and leaders of all organizations in a few short years.

In 2004, Dr. Terri Manning, Director of the Center for Applied Research at Central Piedmont Community College, in Charlotte, North Carolina, and her team, began to study the Millennial Generation and compared it with previous generations. The research first revealed that all generations:

- Consist of approximately a 20-year span (not all demographers and generation researchers agree on the exact start/stop dates)
- Have a unique set of values
- React to the generation before them
- Look at their generation as the standard of comparison
- Look at the next generation skeptically "These kids today..."
- May have a blended set of characteristics if they were born on the "cusp" of their particular generation
- They're either idealistic, reactive, civic or adaptive

The center's study considered economic conditions, societal norms, and political and crises events that occurred during this generation's formative years.

The findings disclosed that the Millennial Generation experienced their parents financial boom of the 1990's, as well as, the loss of their investments (college funds) during the early 2000's; and the ongoing disparity between races.

The research also speaks to the influence of Parental Care during the Millennial era, noting:

- Today's typical family is spending more, not less, time with kids
- Smaller families mean more time with each child.
- Fathers are spending more time with children.
- There is a strong connection between the social lives of parents and kids
- Millennials tend to get along better with their parent's, as young adults, sharing many of their values

The project also showed, that most Millennials:
- Are civic-minded, like the GI Generation
- Are optimistic, long-term planners and high achievers, with reduced rates of violent crime, teen pregnancy, smoking and alcohol use
- Believe they have the potential to be great and probably will. (We expect them to provide us with a new definition of patriotism)
- Will likely be a significant generation philanthropically... and have a desire to "give back"
- Are "master negotiators," who will negotiate with anyone, including parents, teachers and supervisors

Millennials repeatedly demonstrate differences in values from other generations. When purchasing their first home, Millennials will likely ask questions about the "green" aspects of the home. Environment, green and recycling are all topics they've grown up with and are aware of. They are interested in a life with value and meaning, and their aspirations differ significantly from those of the boomer generation.

These differences are critical for organizations to understand, in order to establish *high-performing, tension-free work cultures*, which remain profitable in a competitive marketplace.

For the Millennial Generation, dialogue and two-way communication is imperative. This also holds true for suggestions and feedback. Having grown up with technology, Millennials expect immediate answers at their fingertips. This sense of urgency adds to their expectations, impatience and frustration. They also:

- Demand to know how their work fits into the future scheme of the company
- Expect to work and have fun at the same time
- Look forward to developmental support that will push training and technology to new levels
- Will create a culture of work, characterized by personal independence

Correspondingly good news for employers is that with the right kind of challenge, opportunity, and support, Millennials are likely to be engaged, loyal and dedicated employees.

Aristotle was correct when he said, "Society is something in nature that precedes the individual." It follows that:

- The birth year of your employees drives their core values
- World events over the last 50 years impact employee attitudes and expectations
- Generational membership has consequences for teamwork work relationships, and retention
- Generational values bear on business goals and objectives
- Market reactions to brand and image are influenced by generational membership

These observations alone are compelling, but there is much more to the research findings.

Issues to Prepare For

Organizations would do well to be prepared for challenges posed by this group of people. As they migrate into established businesses, Millenials potentially could be viewed as confrontational, rude, both disrespectful and misunderstood by members of other generations.

The primary reason for this is that Millennials have been taught, and encouraged, to question and negotiate everything. They believe, based on their parent's experiences, not to trust or succumb to blind obedience, just because someone says so.

Remember, these people are the children of parents who were told and believed that if you worked hard and got a good education, you would have a job for life and be able to retire with enough money to maintain a reasonable quality of life. As you're aware, life hasn't quite turned out that way.

A few years ago, when millennial children began entering colleges, administrators were shocked by new students who questioned and tried to negotiate everything. It was reported that this group of students, without a second thought, would confront their professors, challenging due dates posted for term papers and other major projects. Complaints included that certain dates were just not reasonable because they coincided within the same week of the televised American Idol finals.

Remember when companies used to limit the number of personal calls on the company phone? Millennials would rather look for another job if asked to stop texting during working hours. An extreme example of this behavior is the cashier in the store; scanning your groceries with one hand, while texting with their other hand! Uncharacteristic of previous generations, most Millennials feel they should be the *exception,* instead of the *example.*

Because of their hovering protective behavior, millennial parents are often referred to as "helicopter parents." It was reported that beginning in 2004 many colleges decided to conduct separate orientations to keep students and parents apart during the critical period of information distribution and adjustment.

It can be expected that some of these same millennial workers will find traditional entry level jobs unsuitable. With roughly 40% of Millennials in the workplace, as of 2010, HR people have confirmed that new hires, working for fixed periods in a variety of assignments, have been challenging and costly. The rate, at which new hires have been leaving, less than six months after being hired, has been significantly higher than preceding generations.

It would be wise to remember that during most of their lives, everything for Millennials has been "24/7." They are accustomed to having what they want, when they want it and how they want it. Getting them to show up on time and perform as expected is largely a matter of mutual respect. Letting them know you understand and respect their priorities, but at the same time they need to respect yours.

These same Millennials have no patience for decisions based on seniority. They don't understand why a senior manager is given the latest fastest computer, with the newest software they can't even use, while the "new-to-the-workplace millennial techno geeks," have to use old stale technology.

Younger Generation…No Rush to grow Up

To make matters worse, institutions are being confronted with research beginning to show that younger generations are in no hurry to grow up. Leading this research is Frank Furstenberg, from the MacArthur Foundation Research Network on Transitions to Adulthood, (www.macfound.org) a team of scholars who have been studying this phenomenon. "A new period of life is emerging, in which young people are no longer adolescents but not yet adults," he said.

In a 2010 *New York Times*, (www.nytimes.com) story, Patricia Cohen adds to Furstenberg's comments, "National surveys reveal that an overwhelming majority of Americans – including younger adults—agree that between 20 and 22, people should be finished with school, working and living on their own. But in practice, many people in their 20's and early 30's have not yet reached these traditional milestones."

Organizational traditionalists would argue that there will always be challenges, due to personal opinions, in the workplace. The competitive nature of four competing generations is no different. They also suggest that the solution is to simply understand generational differences... which they believe will reduce tensions.

Frank Furstenberg and his team point out the flaw in this traditionalist thinking. His research suggests that the bigger problem for businesses and organizations is that, "We have not developed and strengthened institutions to serve young adults, because we're still living with the archaic idea that people enter adulthood in their late teens or early 20's," Furstenberg says.

A More Optimistic View

Dr. Terri Manning suggests that we look at teachers, leaders and managers occupying the 'power' positions today. She says, "Almost all of these people attended schools where they were taught to become *content* specialists. Today, all the content that anyone could ever want or use is available and accessible from the Internet. Imagine how frustrating it must be for the people in positions of power trying to push their content on those (Millennials) who either already have it or know where to get it from. On the flip side is the frustration felt by Millennials, recognized to be *life-long learners*. They are eager to be mentored in areas of process application, distribution and presentation/success skills."

"A hands-off boss will be totally ineffective working with Millennials. On the other hand, those who recognize, mentor and engage Millennials, for the skills they abound with, ultimately may be responsible for saving these same businesses and organizations from themselves," she says.

Tips To Keep the Fish In *YOUR* Boat

1. Become aware of Millennial core values

2. Harnessing Millennial's energy can be a positive way to add their attributes to the organization

3. Generational membership has consequences for teamwork, work relationships and retention

4. Market reactions to brand and image are also influenced by generational membership

5. Millennials have been taught, based on their parents experience, not to accept blind obedience just because someone says so

6. Competing generational attitudes can be costly, because they raise tension in the workplace and reduce opportunities for outstanding customer experiences

7. While generational insight can help, organizations will need to do more to reduce tension in the workplace

8. The most effective leaders of 'life-long learner' Millennials will harness their energy and enthusiasm; by recognizing, mentoring and engaging them for the skills they abound with

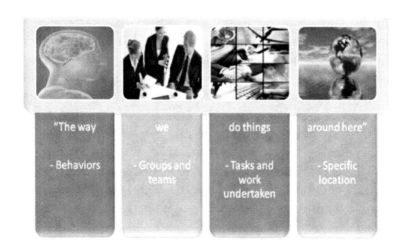

Chapter 13

Corporate Culture…
Defining Performance Success

You would think that the difficulty of attracting and retaining customers, as a result of shifting buyer attitudes and behaviors, would be enough to cause tension in the workplace. However, adding generational diversity to the mix creates another whole dimension. As pointed out in the last chapter, businesses and organizations have never had to deal with (in modern history) four unique generations working side by side, all trying to advance an agenda relevant only to them.

If this has been your experience, you may find it helpful to examine how organizations in general, deal with tensions in the workplace. Most tensions in the workplace are dealt with, by treating the symptoms. Unfortunately, *tensions* are almost always a symptom of an even larger issue, that of *culture* in the workplace.

Culture…Civilization in the Workplace

Regardless of the symptoms, "when faced with tensions inside the organization, many leaders fail to abide by their own mission and vision statements," notes my colleague Dan Kensil, a certified business coach. "These failures destroy the credibility of the leadership. Mission, vision and value statements are only effective when anchored by promised behaviors, coupled to accountability. In the ideal corporate culture, personal agendas are sacrificed on behalf of organizational agendas, and that includes behavior."

When the 2010 recession-plagued economy began to come back, experts said that employers were increasingly concerned about retaining stressed-out employees, who survived layoffs, benefits/pay reductions and increased workloads. Smart employers reviewed their workplace cultures and how they recognized employees; from the structure of rewards programs to telecommuting.

Twenty-eight percent of workers, responding to a 2010 CareerBuilder survey, reported they expect to switch fields, looking for more interesting work, pay, and chances for advancement or stability.

Few would disagree that through conduct, values will influence personal performance and, ultimately, business profitability. Perhaps then, solutions to a variety of problems can be solved by redefining the culture of your organization. Kensil suggests testing the strength of alignment between culture and objectives by leaders asking themselves the following:

Workplace Culture Test

1. Does every member of your stakeholder chain, from your suppliers' vendors, to society as a whole, benefit equally from your commitment of support?

2. Does your organization adhere to, and not simply support, its published mission, vision and value statements?

3. Does your company's value declaration include promised behaviors?

4. Are your company's job descriptions well documented with mission-critical competencies, key performance indicators and incumbent accountabilities?

5. Does your organization employ patterned interviewing and personal coaching in the battle for talent?

6. Has your organization eliminated the fear that prompts wasteful acts of self-preservation?

7. Does your leadership team behave with constancy of purpose?

8. Have the organization's mid- to long-term challenges been identified, along with the competencies and culture needed to exploit those opportunities?

9. Is the leadership team driving to remove hurdles that impede your team's pursuit of performance excellence?

Fortunately, organizations today are able to quantify and qualify their culture by engaging the right consultant/coach who can apply the right tools.

It should be noted, however, that many leaders don't like the culture they have, but they struggle to describe it or specify how they would change it.

Much of this is a labeling problem. The key is approaching the problem with a menu of labels and definitions that accurately describe the desired culture.

Toyota's Culture

In spite of automaker Toyota's, (www.toyota.com) 2010 recall crisis, that organization has exemplified the value of defining culture with precision. It views itself as a manufacturer that "builds cars better," rather than one that "builds better cars." This major distinction drives everything the company does.

Another of Toyota's cultural features is demonstrated in its way-of-life suggestion plan that generates more than one million suggestions per year. Unlike most U.S. manufacturers, Toyota does not reward employees for suggestions with large payments. Neither does it seek the big-breakthrough idea. Instead, Toyota vigorously pursues constant, incremental improvements. And today, at least in the auto industry, it seems the tortoise is winning the race.

Cultural alignment provides Toyota with a unique competitive strategic advantage. The Harbour-Felax Group, (www.linkedin.com/pub/laurie-harbour-felax) a Royal Oak, Michigan consulting company, reported that, "Toyota's costs were $2,400 less per car than Ford, GM and Chrysler, in part through manufacturing efficiencies, over and above labor cost differences, during 2005."

Another example of cultural practices that must not be overlooked is the Nordstrom department store chain. "Nordstrom empowers its employees with the freedom to make decisions, and is willing to live with those decisions. Delegating authority and accountability is the ultimate expression of leadership," say Robert Spector and Patrick D. McCarthy in their book The Nordstrom Way. Admittedly, "working at Nordstrom is not for everybody. Demands and expectations are high. The people who succeed enjoy working in an unrestricted environment, say Spector and McCarthy.

Zappos.com

In Chapter 5, I described a personal experience with a company called zappos.com. The experience was so extraordinary that I was compelled to learn more about them and how they're able to provide the very types of customer experiences that most organizations should emulate, in the future.

Zappos has discovered that it takes a culture, driven by placing the customer at the center of all activity and building around that.

Zappos stated core values begin with:

"As we grow as a company, it has become more and more important to explicitly define the core values from which we develop our culture, our brand, and our business strategies. These are the ten core values that we live by:"

1. Deliver WOW Through Service
2. Embrace and Drive Change
3. Create Fun and A Little Weirdness
4. Be Adventurous, Creative, and Open-Minded
5. Pursue Growth and Learning
6. Build Open and Honest Relationships With Communication
7. Build a Positive Team and Family Spirit
8. Do More With Less
9. Be Passionate and Determined
10. Be Humble

What Others Say About Culture

Ernie Sigmon, president of the Asheville, North Carolina based public relations and communication company, S&S Communications, Inc., (www.linkedin.com-/in/ssvideoconcepts.com) says that, "Culture is equal to building relations, doing the right thing even if you lose money, being honest and not burning bridges is the key to business success. Clients need to be business partners, with names and treated like you want to be treated."

"On a scale of 1 to 10, with 10 being most, *culture* is worth a 10 as it plays in the success of a business or organization," says Thomas Kirkpatrick Owner and Managing Partner, SPG Strategic Partners Group, Inc., (www.spg-group.com) of Greensboro/Winston-Salem, North Carolina.

"Why," Kirkpatrick asks? "Because it is the culture... that lays the foundation for energy and focus in an organization. No matter the talent and structure, the most successful CEO creates and provides the "activity factors" that ignite the forces that result in an environment of excellence. While this seems to be an easy thing to talk about and put on paper; it is exceptionally difficult to do. The difficulty arises when you mix in talent, ego, ambitions, goals and "teamwork" and make it work and make it "the intangible". However, when you achieve a culture sought after, you will have leaders throughout your organization."

Also viewing culture as a "10" is Tom Hamilton, an area manager at Hattrich Enterprises dba CiCi's Pizza, (www.-linkedin.com/companies/hattrichenterprises-dba-cici'spizza) in Charlotte, North Carolina. Hamilton says "It's what guests (customers) can relate to, believe in, and become loyal to. It is inviting them into your concept's way of life and showing them how it impacts them for the better."

Lastly, Renee Cloud, founder of Clerical Business Solutions, Memphis, Tennessee says, "A business culture disables or enables a company to achieve goals, become successful & grow. How a person wants their company culture to perform should be part of their business plan, strategy & strategic planning. A successful company should put forth an effort to insure that their vision for the right company culture is implemented."

Former GE CEO... and Culture

Former General Electric Corp. Chief Executive Jack Welch affirms the importance of culture each time he advises organizations to "never hire people (or acquire companies) whose corporate culture doesn't match your own. No matter how good the numbers look, culture matters as much as financial profile."

So whether your company or organization is large or small, you would be wise to pay rigorous attention to its culture. If for no other reason, your competition may have just gotten interested in the topic.

The Bottom Line of Culture

Intentionally or unintentionally the culture of an organization is the foundation that determines the environment people work in. In the *ideal* environment, as suggested by Dan Kensil, "personal agendas are sacrificed on behalf of organizational agenda... and that includes behavior; that through conduct, values will influence personal performance and, ultimately, business profitability."

Perhaps to summarize, "happy engaged employees usually lead to happy loyal customers."

Tips To Keep the Fish In *YOUR* Boat

1. Tensions in the workplace are symptoms of problems with culture

2. Organizations need to abide by their mission and vision statements

3. Personal agendas should be sacrificed on behalf of organizational agendas, and that includes behavior

4. The strength of alignment between culture and objectives should be tested

5. A glossary of labels and definitions should be created that accurately describes the culture and be stated as what is desired

6. Cultural alignment of all employees keeps everyone on the same page

7. Happy culture… happy employees… happy customers

8. Attention to culture is important, if for no other reason than competition may be paying attention to their culture

Prepare yourself to

Chapter 14

What Got *YOU* Where you Are *TODAY* Won't Take *YOU* Where you Want to Be In the *FUTURE*

A Brief History of Customer Service

As far back as the 1950's, traditional customer service transactions were relegated to "back-room" office functions. Eventually, customer service departments evolved to become sophisticated "call centers." This change happened when senior managers began to equate "happy customers" with profitable new marketing practices. This thinking became popular with names such as *Target Marketing, Individualized Marketing, One-on-one marketing, Customer Care and Relationship Marketing*. Then, beginning around 2000, there was an explosion of *Customer Relationship Management* solutions. Today, there are more than 5,000 different companies offering CRM solutions.

While CRM solutions continue to provide superb intelligence to marketing decision makers, things are markedly different today, compared to last decade. This was validated by Starbucks CEO, Howard Schultz, (www.starbucks.com) in a 2010 *Time Magazine* interview where he said... "People get information in all kinds of ways now and companies can no longer talk *at* the consumer. You have to engage in a discussion and let people create, discover and share information and not just try to sell them things."

The *Customer Experience Report 2008*, from Harris Interactive, (www.harrisinteractive.com) validates Schultz's comments and confirms that "customer experience rules!" They report that "58% of customers recommend and return to companies because of outstanding service."

Today...

Today, most people blame the "economy" for their business' unsuccessful efforts to attract and retain customers. If it were only the economy, organizations could simply wait out the difficult times until the inevitable turn-around. The problem has to do with several compounding factors, not just the economy. In December of 2009, a *Time Magazine* cover story, "The Decade from Hell," attempted to explain, from a news point of view, iconic issues of the decade 2000-2009. The headline subtitle, "And why the next one will be better," suggested that an economic recovery would occur.

What *Time Magazine* and others may have missed, is that the economy was only one factor. There are, in fact, many that have contributed to why the marketplace is where it is, today. They include:
- The 9/11 terrorist attack
- The economic crisis/recession
- The banking crisis
- The mortgage crisis
- The housing crisis
- The unemployment crisis
- Conflicting environmental policy (crisis)
- Competing generational attitudes
- Technology
- Social media

Most experts believe the above factors are the primary causes for the shift in buyer attitudes and behaviors. What's more is that the pervasiveness of this phenomenon has impacted every market in the United States. This reality cannot be overstated. Leaders and managers need to rethink everything they have ever learned about marketing and customer service, in order for their organizations to be more effective.

From a sociological and business perspective, there is one overriding theme or message; "What got you where you are today is unlikely to take you where you want to be in the future."

A New Holy Grail for Business

Encouragingly, there are strategies, if implemented carefully that offer the best opportunities for survival, growth and success in the future.

Pull vs. *Push* Marketing and Sales

In his book, *Midas Marketing*, (www.midasnation.com) author Rob Slee, writes, "For many years, organizations have misunderstood the differences between *marketing* and *sales;* even misusing vocabulary to insinuate that they are the same. Marketing is a strategic function, while selling is a tactical function. That could be a big reason why organizations that have VP's of Sales and Marketing are operating with a contradiction of terminology. In actuality, even if it was possible, the title would have to be, VP of Marketing and Sales."

He also suggests the eventual extinction of most sales people, as we know them today, is a certainty. "Pulling the customer with a compelling value proposition is the single most critical force a company must generate. This contrasts sharply with the pushing force that has characterized businesses in the past. Historically, businesses created a product or service, hired a bunch of sales people and used them to push the product onto the market. However, the Internet has become the great equalizer. It has changed the rules of buying; making the old model highly inefficient. With the Internet, you can post your value proposition for billions to see. This quickly allows buyers to shop and buy the competitive offering the best value proposition," says Slee. Assuming Slee is correct, then most organizations will need to transform from *push*, to both *pull marketing* and *pull* sales strategies, in order to survive and flourish in the future.

The need for rethinking and transforming marketing and sales strategy should be apparent today. The overly aggressive sales person, who has been trained to "attack" the customer and "force" a purchase decision, has probably noticed their efforts having the opposite effect, pushing prospects away instead.

How to "Pull" Rather than "Push"

My colleague, Peter Popovich, (www.linkedin.com/in/-peterpopovich) is an executive coach. His motto is

"Transforming Lives Daily," and he strongly agrees with Slee about the need for businesses to stop pushing and to do more pulling. Popovich suggests that people begin this process first by considering the sphere of their own personal experience. He says, "Ask yourself, from your own perspective as a consumer, customer, prospect, business owner, manager, patient, fan, donor, member, patron or employee; Which do you find more effective... being pummeled, prodded and pushed into a purchase decision? Or, to be authentically empowered, engaged, respected and pulled into a purchase decision? The answer is obvious. The process is not. How then? ...By having leaders that effectively modify their cultures."

What's more, "These same questions can be asked by people in virtually every size organization, across every industry segment and applies equally to both for-profits and nonprofits," says Popovich.

For years, business schools have taught that it costs 10 times more to sell a new customer than it does to keep an existing one. With what we now know, it's well past time that business owners, chief executives, executive directors and managers start practicing this lesson for the sake of their organizations.

Furthermore, converting from push to pull strategies doesn't need to be costly. Organizations, not already doing so, can begin a time sensitive transition effort to phase in marketing and sales strategies that "pull" customers and reduce efforts that "push" customers to make purchase decisions.

A different way to think and behave for success

Another strategy for success is one that helps brand and differentiate products and services... providing **outstanding, extraordinary, incredible customer experiences.**

Providing this type of customer experience may be difficult for some organizations. The difficulty is a "cultural" one. Many organizations have undefined cultures. That is to say, limited or no stated rules or boundaries that can be used to specify what the culture is supposed to be. Others offer *some* cultural definition, however, in many cases the definition is in conflict with their purpose. There are organizations that, by their culture, present obstacles to providing a level of customer experience that would help them the most.

These organizations have silos, fiefdoms, politics, egos, policies, fear factors and bureaucracy that get in the way. Frequently, mission, vision and value statements are out of alignment, or may even conflict with the purpose of the organization. In those instances, you can be sure that the employees are out of alignment with the purpose as well. Lastly, there are managers and employees who are not held responsible for cross functional relationships. Does any of this sound familiar?

To further complicate matters, there are impatient executives, who *want* their customers to have outstanding experiences, however, don't know what to do first. Without taking the time, there will be many who jump to solutions, doing more harm than good.

The encouraging news is that organizational change is possible. No one should ever suggest that change will be easy. It seldom is!

Business leaders would be mistaken to think that they can simply demand or mandate their organization to begin providing outstanding experiences to customers.

I recognize that senior managers often desire to be perceived as sincere, however, sincerity is seldom a prominent factor in business success. Profit margins, strategies, tactics and behavior are. Yes, intention matters, although walking-the-walk and talking-the-talk is the most effective way to get there. Anything short of this will only derail the process. Providing an outstanding customer experience first requires a look at your *current* situation. After that, you can develop a plan, focusing on customer centricity.

Following is a guide that may provide some help. (NOTE - In most cases using a facilitator, consultant or business coach, who offers "fresh eyes," can shorten the process, mediate turf battles and keep the process on track.)

Guide to Providing an *Outstanding Customer Experience*

1. Begin by avoiding the tendency to jump to solutions. A "quick fix" will jeopardize efficiency, effectiveness, profitability and the creation and maintenance of an extraordinary customer experience.

    - Look at *What* needs to happen... Then *How*
    - Look at your entire customer contact scale... then, and only then, address the *how*

2. Everyone in the organization MUST own a piece of the customer experience
    - Mission, vision and values should be audited, to be sure they accurately define the purpose of the organization
    - Align employees to be on-purpose with organizational goals
    - Include all customer "touch points" and activities
    - Question everything... Previous management decisions, silos, fiefdoms, politics, fear factors and all bureaucracy
    - Make employees responsible for cross-functional relationships

3. Survey and listen to customers frequently
    - Remember that while most customers are eager to give advice, they also frequently consider where else they can purchase the product or service

4. Create a new culture with rules

- Align the organization around the customer
- Make sure employees, processes and technology carry out the business' CUSTOMER CENTRIC MISSION
- Create and deliver a constant experience
- Interactivity is key to maintaining relationships

5. Measure results
   - Use scorecards for employees, departments and staff members
   - Assign specific objectives and key performance indicators
   - Review results on a monthly basis, focusing on improvement, not punishment

It is precisely this type of customer experience that will not only get the fish to swim to *you*, but also keep them in *your* boat.

How Social Media Networking Can Help

According to PR technology expert Drew Gerber, (www.pitchrate.com), "Social networking is about building community. Think about the kinds of people and businesses you gravitate toward in your own personal social networking experience. Whose tweets do you follow? What pages are you a fan of in FaceBook?"

So what are they doing to engage you? "Most likely they're using social networking as a platform to develop relationships with their customers and potential clients, NOT necessarily to sell their product. It's a common misstep people make when they dive into FaceBook, Twitter or LinkedIn... over-promotion. Tweets can just be links to your website, sales page or shopping cart. You have to provide value and engage people online just as you would if you were building a business relationship in person. If someone comes in and all they want to do is promote, promote, promote, that approach is likely to go nowhere. You have to look at social networking as a platform where you can answer questions, provide quality customer service and valuable information, and as a place where you can listen to your target market's concerns. You have your website and/or storefront to sell things; your social networking should be about building community, not sales," says Gerber.

Social Media and Customer Service

Historically, when customers were unhappy with the way they were treated by a business, they would make a telephone call to the manager or write an angry letter. Today, even sharp rebuking emails are becoming passé. Tech savvy consumers are beginning to grasp that the easiest and fastest way to have their complaint heard and resolved is to use the power and speed of Twitter.

Many customer service experts suggest that it's the instant public humiliation that makes Twitter grievances unique. "Until now, most customer service has been a black hole of obscurity," says Pete Blackshaw, author of, *Satisfied Customers Tell Three Friends, Angry Customers Tell 3,000*, (www.tell3000.editspot.com). "Now you just spend a few minutes searching tweets to see who's mad and then how they were dealt with."

Social Media and "Pull" Strategies

There has never been a greater facilitator of "pull" strategies and opportunities to provide an outstanding customer experience than that of the Internet and correspondingly, social media.

The Internet is the great equalizer. It levels the playing field for everyone. With a professional presence, a small business can make as powerful an impression and have as lengthy a reach, as the largest name brand organization.

Social media guru, Ira Bass, (www.IBMedia.biz), suggests that, "social media, with its no cost (for media) pricing model, enables anyone to post messages that literally billions of people can (be pulled in) to respond to." Bass has also observed that, "many people who don't utilize marketing as an essential aspect of their business, seem to be struggling with using social media. Those who recognize marketing's importance are going for it. They're thinking outside the box, experimenting, trying a variety of different tactics and going with the ones that are most effective. Conversely, the more conservative an organization is, the more likely they will apply traditional corporate models that keep them inside the box." Remember what T. Boone Pickens says, "Do something...what's the worst that could happen? You'd be wrong?" <u>Bass warns however that</u>, "the *Field of Dreams* model, "if <u>you build it, they will come;" does not apply to social media. They will only come if what is created remains relevant, interesting and dynamic."</u>

The following is an example that personifies the use of pull vs. push, changes to culture and using the Internet/social media to provide outstanding customer experiences.

The Charlotte Fire Department

One municipally owned organization, which is ahead of the curve for recognizing *where they want to be in the future,* is the 123 year old, Charlotte Fire Department (CFD), (www.charmeck.org) in Charlotte, North Carolina. The CFD has been able to formulate a culture, enabling them to become a practitioner of providing outstanding customer experiences. This has been done without jeopardizing their primary first-responder purpose.

Fire Chief Jon Hannan, leader of the eleven hundred plus employee agency, has encouraged a culture of engagement, transparency and communication-immediacy, that has raised the bar and has become a model for what a first-responder organization can do.

Public Information Officers (PIO) Captain Rob Brisley and Captain Mark Basnight, encouraged by Chief Hannan, led a 2009 effort to improve communication with their customers. This effort resulted in their department winning the prestigious PIO Social Media Responder of the Year Award.

Basnight and Brisley used social media to transform information distribution to the department's customers. Brisley says, "Historically, we relied on time consuming phone calls, press releases, fax distribution and tomorrow's news media outlets, to communicate our message. Basnight adds, "social media networks, like FaceBook, Twitter and LiveJournal, enable us to bring a level of immediacy to our information and messages, which were never before imagined." The use of social media and its immediacy has helped CFD broaden their customer base. Brisley says, "Both low priority safety information and high priority emergency information is now equally available, based upon our customer's time frames and preferences."

Brisley also proudly reports, that his partner, Basnight, has created an integrated platform of social media sites, making it easier to distribute and monitor information through the most effective channels. This allows the right message to get to the right constituency in a timely fashion (i.e. other first responder agencies, media and the public), making life easier and better for all of the stakeholders.

Tips for Getting the Fish to Swim to *YOU* & Keeping Them in *YOUR* Boat

1. Recognize why customer service practices today, *must* be different than the past

2. CHOICE, COMPLEXITY and CHANGE are compelling enough reasons for everyone to think and behave differently

3. "Pull" marketing and sales strategies will increasingly be more successful than traditional "push" strategies

4. Providing an outstanding customer experience offers the greatest opportunity to help brand and differentiate products and services

5. Making changes to culture takes time, planning and careful execution

6. Following a guide, and using an outside consultant as "fresh eyes," can be helpful and effective toward getting repositioned for this new age

7. Social media may be the most effective tool to resolve customer complaints

8. Social networking should be used as a platform to develop relationships with their customers and potential clients, NOT necessarily to sell their product

Chapter 15

The Value of Internal Customer Experiences

At this point, I am almost apologetic to suggest, that none of the previous fourteen chapters in this book will be of much value if appropriate attention is not given to the value of "internal customer experiences."

The coach of any team sport will tell you that a mediocre team with the right attitude, usually wins, over a physically stronger team with a bad attitude.

The selection of the *right* people is critical, as discussed in chapter 11, "The Right Employees Make All the Difference." However, if the environment inside the organization is poisoned by conflicted mission, core value or purpose statements…even the *right* employees will find it difficult to maintain the ship. If they don't leave first, those same employees will often sabotage efforts to provide outstanding (external) customer experiences. Many managers avoid dealing with internal customer issues. You don't have to make this mistake.

The Danger of Double Standards

It seems ironic to me how often a leader will hire a consultant to help the organization in one area, only to find the real problem, is in another area. This is often the case when management states what they expect of employees, in terms of behavior; then act as if the rules only apply to some. All the employee recognition programs or 401 K's offered will not solve a turnover problem when the issues have to do with management behavior. Consistency is the key to solving this problem.

A client complained of difficulty retaining employees, past the six month mark. He explained that it was costly for the company to train new people, only to have them quit, along with taking corporate secrets with them. So, he asked my firm to create a compensation program designed to incent employee loyalty and keep new hires with his company, for a reasonable length of time.

During the second week of the assignment, we began to observe the owner/president's body-language and behavior, regarding a specific female employee. We also observed that the two arranged to have lunch together almost every day and frequently left together several times over the course of the week, not returning until the next day. It soon became clear following discussions with other employees, that it was the behavior of the owner/president that was causing the turnover problem, rather than the lack of a retention program.

Or how about the "male dominated" company, where the owner arranges weekly golf outings with his predominantly male sales staff… during working hours. If you think this will go unnoticed with the remaining office staff, think again.

When Credentials Are Not Enough

I recently observed a department with low morale, probably related to the manager/supervisor's people skills. She didn't acknowledge or interact with the employees. (This manager is the same person who posts mission, vision and core value statements regarding the need for employees to demonstrate respect to individuals.) When the department is shorthanded, the manager is never one to pitch in and help. This discourages the employees further, since it suggests their boss doesn't have a clue as to what goes on in their respective areas. This is the same manager who never recognizes good work or extra effort, instead only has words for subordinates when they have done something wrong.

In this case, the person may have the "paper" credentials to manage but lacks the people skills necessary to operate successfully in the environment. As an outsider I had lots of questions in my mind about who is responsible for managing the manager. A situation like this begs for a review. Courses of action might include, additional training as well as changes to the culture, encouraging quality *internal* customer experiences.

Internal Policy and Communications

Following recurring requests, senior management agreed to allow their eighty-five employees to dress "business casual" on Fridays.

This change in policy was never discussed or explained, rather simply announced. On the first Friday of the new policy, some employees were dressed consistent with what is considered "business casual." Others wore shorts, blue jeans and tee-shirts with varying messages and holes throughout. Additionally, on this Friday, an important customer was expected to tour the facility. Senior management went crazy sending offensive employees home who were not dressed to their satisfaction or expectation.

Most people have a hard time reading minds and predicting the future. Spare the frustrations and embarrassments...clearly and carefully explain policies so NOT to be misunderstood or misinterpreted.

Employee Recognition

ALWAYS acknowledge your employees. This sounds simple but often goes overlooked.

If employees are working extended hours or weekends, during a particular busy time for your business, reward them afterwards. Always let them know how much their hard work and effort is appreciated.

If the owner or senior managers decide to leave at noon every Friday, then announce that the office will close at noon every Friday during the summer. If closing this way isn't possible unilaterally, then offer rotating half days off between employees. A small gesture of goodwill goes a long way.

Employee gifts, movie tickets, restaurant gift cards, etc., are always appreciated. But get ready for trouble in the workplace when one person is singled out as an "outstanding" employee. Somebody will always come up with a reason why they deserved it more. To create balance and equality in the workplace, the perks need to be given to all who made reaching the objective possible.

Beyond tangible recognition efforts, are those that let employees know that you care about related issues, which may concern them.

Think about this: *Employees may not like every decision that is made;* however, bringing them into the process (when possible) lets them have an appreciation for the elements that were considered to reach that decision.

Studies indicate that top talent will begin searching for new opportunities if they do not feel valued and/or engaged in the work place. So it is never too late to take a good look at your corporate culture. Is it what it should be? Are employees engaged? What do they think? One way to engage employees is to ASK them what they think. In this situation, hiring a third party is critical, because it insures honest, straightforward responses.

Too many organizations try to hype the tangible employee recognition programs…be careful of *over* recognition.

I actually know of one company that gives out a $100 monthly bonus to every employee who shows up on time and doesn't miss a day's work, during the month….isn't that what employees are hired to do in the first place?

Additionally, I guarantee your employees won't appreciate that large extravagant holiday party, you threw for them in December…only to be told in January, there will be no salary increases this coming year.

Employees are the "face" of most organizations. As the face, they control most customer touch points; sales, service, support, shipping, accounting, billing, collecting etc. Can an organization ever hope to have outstanding "external" customer experiences without having outstanding "internal" customer experiences, first?

Tips for Getting the Fish to Swim to *YOU* & Keeping Them in *YOUR* Boat

1. Outstanding *internal* customer experiences are a prerequisite for outstanding *external* customer experiences

2. Maintaining double standards demonstrates a breach in organizational culture

3. Today, people skills, across the organization, are imperative to having a successful business

4. Clearly communicate changes in company policy to avoid frustration, tension and misunderstandings

5. Employee recognition is important, however, must be managed with great sensitivity

6. Effective managers let employees know when they do things well AND not so well

In Conclusion

This book contains more than one-hundred sixty examples of what can be done, and more than eighty examples of what not to do, to diminish the effects of choice, complexity and change in this era of transformed buyer attitudes and behaviors.

Converting to *pull* rather than *push* strategies, and providing outstanding customer experiences, will undoubtedly become prevailing ways for the most successful organizations to do business in the future.

There is also an urgent necessity for cultural audits and alignment.

I believe that the most profound outcomes can be achieved by those organizations that combine the concepts above. In addition, reducing emphasis on *how they are doing today* and sharpening the focus on *how they could be doing if they* exercised their potential.

Most organizations make decisions based on the *passion of intuition*. I urge this to be complimented with *the rigor of evidence*.

With this kind of fundamental forward rethinking; organizations, stockholders and stakeholders will celebrate increased returns on investment, along with engaged-dedicated employees and loyal-profitable customers.

Acknowledgments

I am grateful and wish to acknowledge the many individuals and businesses/organizations whose names were mentioned in this book. Many were interviewed, while others served as role models/examples of what can be done using "outside-the-box" thinking, in this age of choice, complexity and change.

They include:

Alemite www.alemite.com	Page 28
Amazon.com www.amazon.com	Page 1, 2
American Express www.americanexpress.com	Pages 23, 24
American Red Cross www.Americanredcross.com	Page 33
Andre Gien, Global Financial Bridge LLC www.gfbridge.com	Back Cover
Ann Michaels and Associates www.ishopforyou.com	Page 36
Apple Computer, Inc www.apple.com	Page 2, 15
Bank of America www.bankofamerica.com	Page 42
BMW www.bmwusa.com	Page 17
Charlotte Fire Department www.charmeck.org	Page 96, 97

Clerical Business Solutions	Page 84, 85
Dan Kensil	Page 80, 81
Drew Gerber www.pitchrate.com	Page 94, 95
Entrepreneur Magazine www.entrepreneur.com	Page 2
Golling Chrysler/Jeep/Dodge www.gollingchryslerjeepdodge.com	Page 57
Harbour-Felax Group www.linkedin.com/pub/laurie-harbour-felax	Page 82
Harris Interactive www.harrisinteractive.com	Page 88
Hattrich Enterprises DBA CiCi's Pizza www.linkedin.com/companies/hattrich-enterprises-dba-cici'spizza	Page 84
Information Industry Association, (now known as Software & Information Industry Assoc.) www.siia.net	Page 7
Integra Staffing & Search www.integrastaffing.com	Page 68
Ira Bass/IBMedia.biz www.ibmedia.biz	Page 95, 96
Jerry Lewis, Detroit Tigers www.detroit.tigers.mlb.com	Back Cover
J. D. Powers and Associates www.jdpower.com	Page 23

Jim Collins, Author of, *Good to Great* www.jimcollins.com	Page 29, 65, 66
Jim Kothe www.sharpenyourmessage.com	Pages 11, 12
Ken Blanchard, Co-Author of, *The One Minute Manager* www.kenblanchard.com	Page iv
Lev Grossman, Time Magazine www.time.com/time/magazine	Page 2
Lincoln-Mercury www.lincolnmercury.com	Page 27
The Living History Program© www.livinghistoryprogram.com	Page 20
Livingston & Haven www.lhtech.com	Page 22, 23
MacArthur Foundation Research Network www.macfound.org	Page 76, 77
Mercedes Benz www.mbusa.com	Page 17
Microsoft Corporation www.microsoft.com	Page 15
Morris-Jenkins www.morrisjenkins.com	Page 66, 67
Netflix www.Netflix.com	Page 2
New York Times www.nytimes.com	Page 76

Nordstrom www.nordstrom.com	Pages 36, 67, 82,
Novant Health www.novanthealth.org	Page 20
Overhead Door Company of Charlotte www.ohdcharlotte.com	Page 67, 68
Pandora Radio www.pandora.com	Page 2
Pete Blackshaw www.tell3000.editspot.com	Page 95
Peter Popovich, Coach www.linkedin.com/in/peterpopovich	Page 90, 91
Process Performance Group, (PPG) www.teletracker.net	Pages 56, 57
Rob Slee, Author of *Midas Marketing* www.midasnation.com	Page 89, 90
San Diego Padres www.padres.com	Page 34, 35
Sheena S. Iyanger, Author of *The Art of Choosing* www.theartofchoosing.com	Page 1
S&S Communications www.linkedin.com/in/ssvideoconcepts.com	Page 84
Signature Healthcare www.signaturehealthcare.org	Page 20
SPG, Strategic Partners Group, Inc. www.spg-group.com	Page 84

Stan Rapp & Tom Collins, Authors of *The Great Marketing Turnaround* www.allbusiness.com	Pages 8, 9
Starbucks Coffee Company www.starbucks.com	Page 88
Sudler & Hennessey Worldwide www.sudler.com	Page 7, 8
Terri Manning, Dr. Central Piedmont Community College www.cpcc.edu	Page 72-74, 77
Time Magazine www.time.com/time/magazine	Pages 3, 88, 89
TiVo www.tivo.com	Page 2
Toyota www.toyota.com	Page 82, 83
Tropical Foods www.tropicalfoods.com	Page 29
Walmart www.Walmart.com	Page 2
Warner Lambert/Pfizer www.pfizer.com	Page 7
YouTube www.youtube.com	Page 2
Zappos.com www.zappos.com	Pages 37, 83